Room Tone

DISTANZ

Room Tone

Rosa Aiello
with Helin Çelik, Beatrice Gibson,
Yaniya Lee, and Ivana Mladenović

KONTEXT

Contents

Editor's Note
Matthias Kliefoth, Theresa Roessler

The gaze through the lens constitutes more than an image; it emerges within social relations. What unfolds in the act of film-making exceeds what is ultimately seen and heard. It is shaped by the dynamics among those present, by hierarchies that are reinforced, resisted, or reimagined in the process of thinking and working together.

Room Tone starts from this premise: that the making of a film may be as significant as—if not more than—the film itself. Filmmaking, in this sense, is not merely capturing something through a lens; rather, it takes place among people, within real, constructed, or reenacted settings that generate shared experiences; or to put it differently, those ideas of "reality" and "fiction" are invited to lose their clear outlines.

The filmmakers brought together in this book by artist Rosa Aiello share a commitment to questioning notions of authorship and the politics of representation. Their reflections circle around authenticity and truth—not as a stable quality, but as something negotiated within relationships. How does one build a relationship? What kind of tool might a camera become in that case? And what does it mean to allow the person being filmed to form a relationship with their own image?

In the context of film productions, room tone is defined as the "neutral silence" recorded on set in the absence of dialogue. Each room and configuration of bodies is recorded separately, since there is a particular quality to the way the walls and physical masses cause the air in the room to vibrate. The silence is never empty. It holds an atmosphere, a tension, a residue of presence. Within Rosa Aiello's inquiry, room tone might become something different: the condition that makes collective work possible—perhaps the subtle cohesion that binds a community through devotion and recognition. It is here that filmmaking shifts from an act of depiction to a practice of listening. Using reality to tell fiction becomes a method. To be present, to remain attuned: these gestures form the texture of a practice that reconsiders not only how films are made, but how belonging and place might be constituted through the act of seeing and being seen.

Alongside contributions by filmmakers Beatrice Gibson, Helin Çelik, and Ivana Mladenović that respond to Rosa Aiello's prompt, *Room Tone* includes a newly commissioned essay by writer and critic Yaniya Lee. The essay engages with Rosa Aiello's films presented in her exhibition *A Good Reputation* at Westfälischer Kunstverein (2025/26) and discusses her ongoing interest in methodology and collaborative work.

Room Tone reflects different methods of documentary and experimental filmmaking as a relational and collaborative practice—"allowing life to occur around it," as Rosa Aiello aptly puts it. As part of the *Kontext* series, the book situates this practice within a broader inquiry into the circumstances, relations, and settings in which work comes into being.

Paradoxical spaces often prove to be the most generative; spaces in which roles and hierarchies are both defined and undone, in which control and openness cohabit, and where meaning emerges not despite, but through these tensions.

Cinema as a Space of Being-With Helin Çelik

As a Kurdish artist, my practice is rooted in exploring women's experiences within geographies of political struggle, creating spaces where their voices, memories, and perspectives can emerge and be shared. Working closely with women who have lived through trauma, I approach filmmaking as a collaborative process that challenges conventional notions of authorship and representation. Through participatory methods, I seek to dissolve the boundaries between filmmaker and subject, opening up collective forms of storytelling and self-expression. By weaving together documentary and narrative elements, I examine the intersections of political and cinematographic memory, where personal histories merge with new visual grammars.

I would like to begin my text with an example drawn from the relational work with one of the main protagonists of my latest feature film, *ANQA* (2023).

After the Jordanian Ministry of Social Affairs declined our request to film in the only women's prison in Amman—an institution where the majority of inmates are not offenders but women seeking protection from so-called honor crimes—my co-producer and I were compelled to reconsider our approach and to seek alternative ways of reaching women who had escaped such circumstances. This proved to be a difficult and delicate process. After extensive research, and with the support of local fixers, we were eventually able to locate several women who were living in hiding in different parts of the country. This is when we met Iman.

Iman was living in a small village in rural Jordan. She had endured an extremely difficult life marked by repeated violence, had often been close to death, and was recently diagnosed with paranoid schizophrenia.

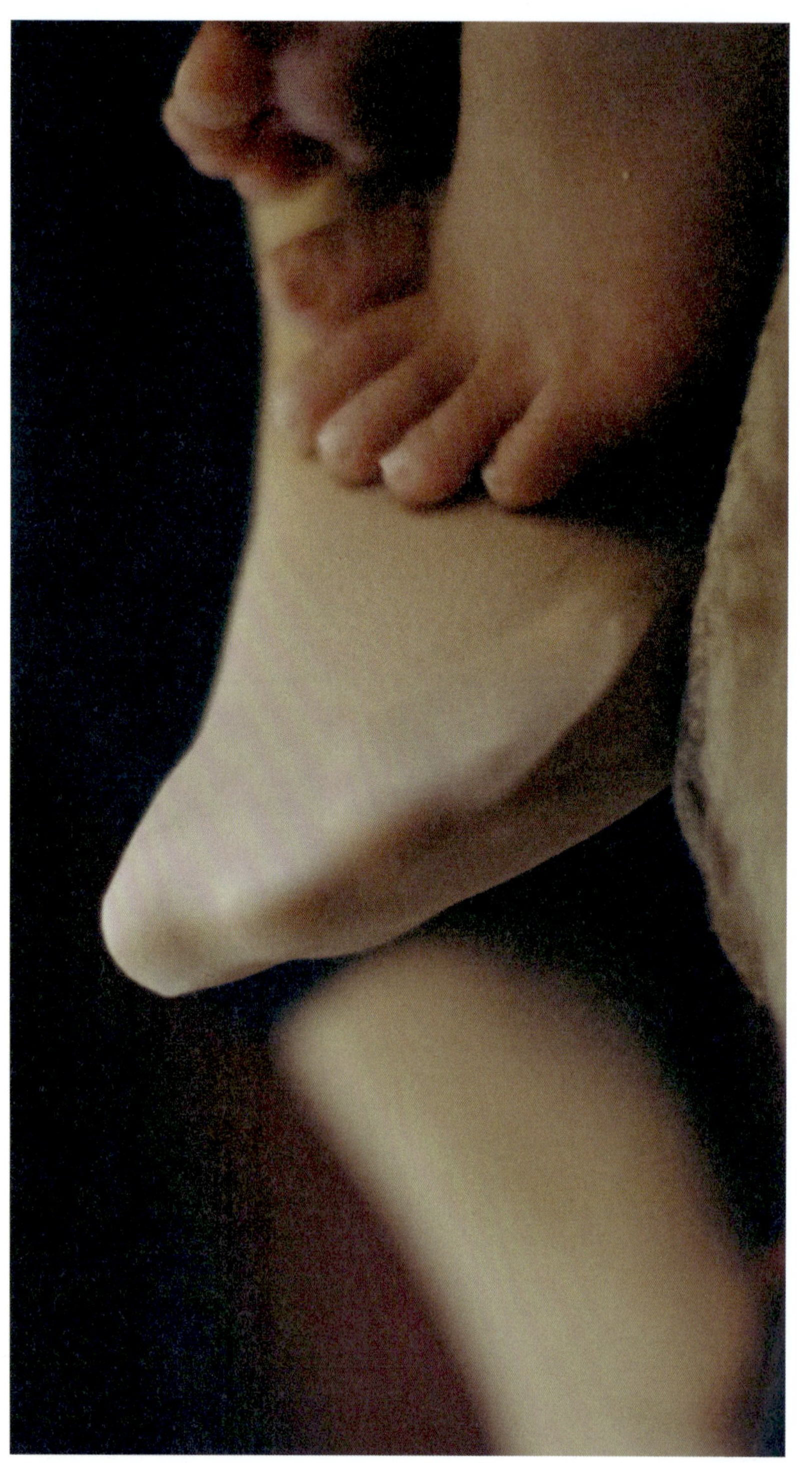

When we met, she was living in almost complete isolation with her four children. Over the course of two years, I visited her often, and after some time, we decided together to make a film about her story. We agreed that her experiences deserved to be heard. I worked with her alongside a very small film crew: three people I had chosen with great care, with a particular emphasis on political awareness and ethical sensitivity, among other things. The team consisted of cinematographer Raquel Fernández Núñez, camera assistant and sound recordist Maitane Carballo Alonso, and myself.

At the beginning of the filmmaking process with Iman, there was a palpable presence of grief, pain, uncertainty, pressure, and loneliness. She felt entirely at the mercy of her daily circumstances and her psychological condition. The space for hope and joy was extremely limited, and her connection to herself and her life had been deeply buried. Her feelings, memories, and experiences were marked by trauma and profound wounds.

In the contexts of the Global South, from which my narratives and subjects originate, violence manifests not only through state policies and the conditions of daily life but also through cinematic representation itself. Within such geographies, the question of how to depict violence without reproducing it becomes a central ethical and aesthetic concern.

For me, it is crucial to resist the reiteration of violence in the act of storytelling, particularly when rearticulating historical and contemporary cinematic narratives. In the field of documentary filmmaking, this entails an ethical responsibility to avoid subjecting individuals—especially those who have already experienced trauma—to renewed symbolic or visual violation through the cinematic gaze.[1]

Mainstream documentary cinema, however, often continues to operate within an informational paradigm, reducing complex lived realities to forms of data or spectacle. My own practice seeks to move beyond this tendency through an approach I describe as “cinematic justice.” This framework aligns with a haptic understanding of cinema—one that privileges sensory engagement and embodied perception over detached observation.

As Laura U. Marks suggests, “haptic visuality” invites a tactile and affective proximity between viewer and image, enabling an encounter that is felt rather than merely seen.[2] In this sense, a cinema that refuses

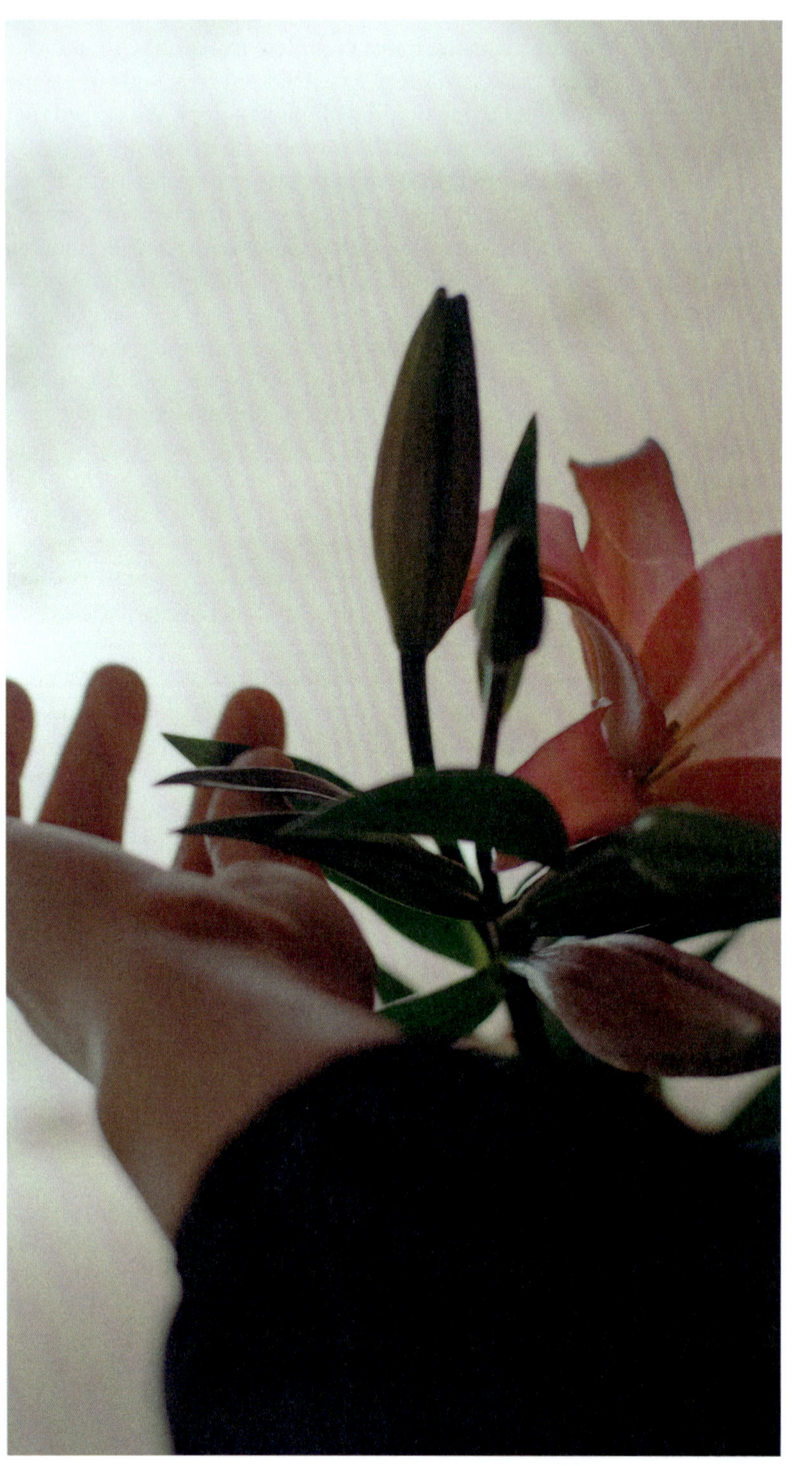

to reproduce violence offers its subjects what the Abounaddara Film Collective calls "the right to the dignified image."[3]

In a cinema where information is absent—or where what exists is fragmented and disjointed—another dimension of perception opens. Such absence enables new forms of understanding. Silence and not-knowing allow us to see—and to re-see—spaces, places, and people. The "haptic image" activates a bodily mode of perception, in which physical and affective contact become possible and another kind of seeing emerges. This way of looking allows us to encounter the subjects on screen not through dates, numbers, or crimes, but through sensation, empathy, and presence—perhaps in a more profoundly human way. It grants them the right to exist beyond the categories of victimhood or crime. This is what I understand as the dignified image.

Rather than approaching the violent experiences of my protagonists through an investigative or judicial lens, I aim to construct a cinematic space that mediates the political through the personal—by observing the everyday lives of those shaped by trauma. Such a practice seeks to restore agency to participants by facilitating reciprocal observation: a process in which they, too, bear witness to us and to the shared conditions that constitute our collective existence. In this mode, cinema becomes not a site of extraction, but of encounter.

I also work as an art therapist in a clinical context, which influences my filmic practice. Both involve the creation of a shared, dialogical space: in filmmaking, this space emerges between filmmaker and protagonist—a relational field in which observation flows in both directions. This dynamic resonates with D. W. Winnicott's concept of "potential space": a transitional zone between inner and outer realities where creativity, healing, and transformation can take place.[4] Within this shared cinematic environment, both filmmaker and participant engage in a process of mutual reflection and emotional co-regulation. This act of co-creation becomes a practice of resilience that allows participants to reframe trauma through narrative reconstruction and symbolic expression.

Drawing on Judith Herman's notion of trauma recovery as a process of safety, remembrance, and reconnection, the filmmaking space can operate as a form of collective therapy, in which the articulation of experience is both witnessed and shared.[5]

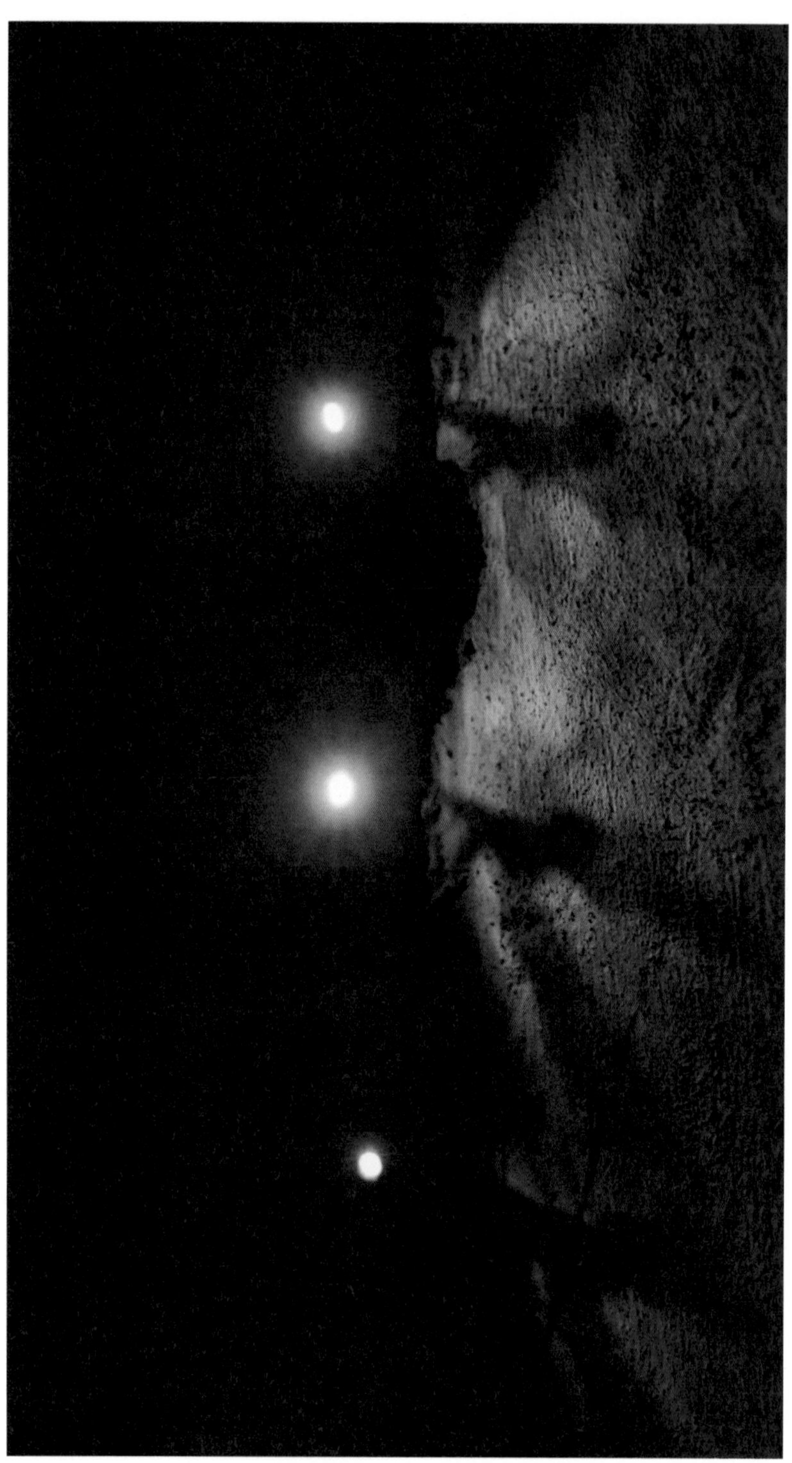

Similarly, Jessica Benjamin's theory of "mutual recognition" offers a framework for understanding how both filmmaker and subject participate in the process of acknowledging each other's subjectivity, thereby transforming hierarchical structures of authorship into collaborative ones.[6] Through this reciprocal process of witnessing, growth occurs on both sides: the participants reclaim agency and voice, while the filmmaker's gaze becomes increasingly self-reflexive and ethically attuned.

The traces of this psychological co-evolution are inscribed in the images themselves. The camera becomes a mediator of presence, intimacy, and repair, its texture shaped by the emotional interplay between those behind and before it. The resulting filmic language carries the imprint of shared resilience and transformation.

The extreme close-up of Iman's face in *ANQA* exemplifies this process. When I first told Raquel, my cinematographer, that I wanted her to position the camera so close to the protagonist, she initially questioned the decision, both aesthetically and ethically. She asked whether I could truly imagine such an image on the big screen and whether it was appropriate to approach the protagonist with such proximity. This led to a collaborative process between the three of us: Raquel, Iman, and me. We experimented with different framings and shared the results with Iman at each stage, showing her precisely how close the camera would come to her face.

Eventually, Iman and I decided together on the close-up, a decision that in turn encouraged Raquel, who would have to operate the camera at that intimate distance for an extended period of filming. It was a bold choice, one that all of us were uncertain about at first. Yet, through ongoing communication, mutual trust, and what I would describe as a form of sisterhood, we were able to make it possible. We empowered one another to embrace this daring approach, and ultimately, this image became the film's signature shot. The decision to film at such proximity represents, on one hand, our emotional and physical closeness, and on the other, what gives the film its distinctive aesthetic language.

During my time with Iman, I perceived that she was trapped, both psychologically and verbally, in recurring phrases that reflected wounds from the past, as well as entrenched beliefs and life patterns. Her psychic confinement affected me profoundly. At times, I felt overwhelmed by waves of sorrow. Remaining fully present in the role of the filmmaker

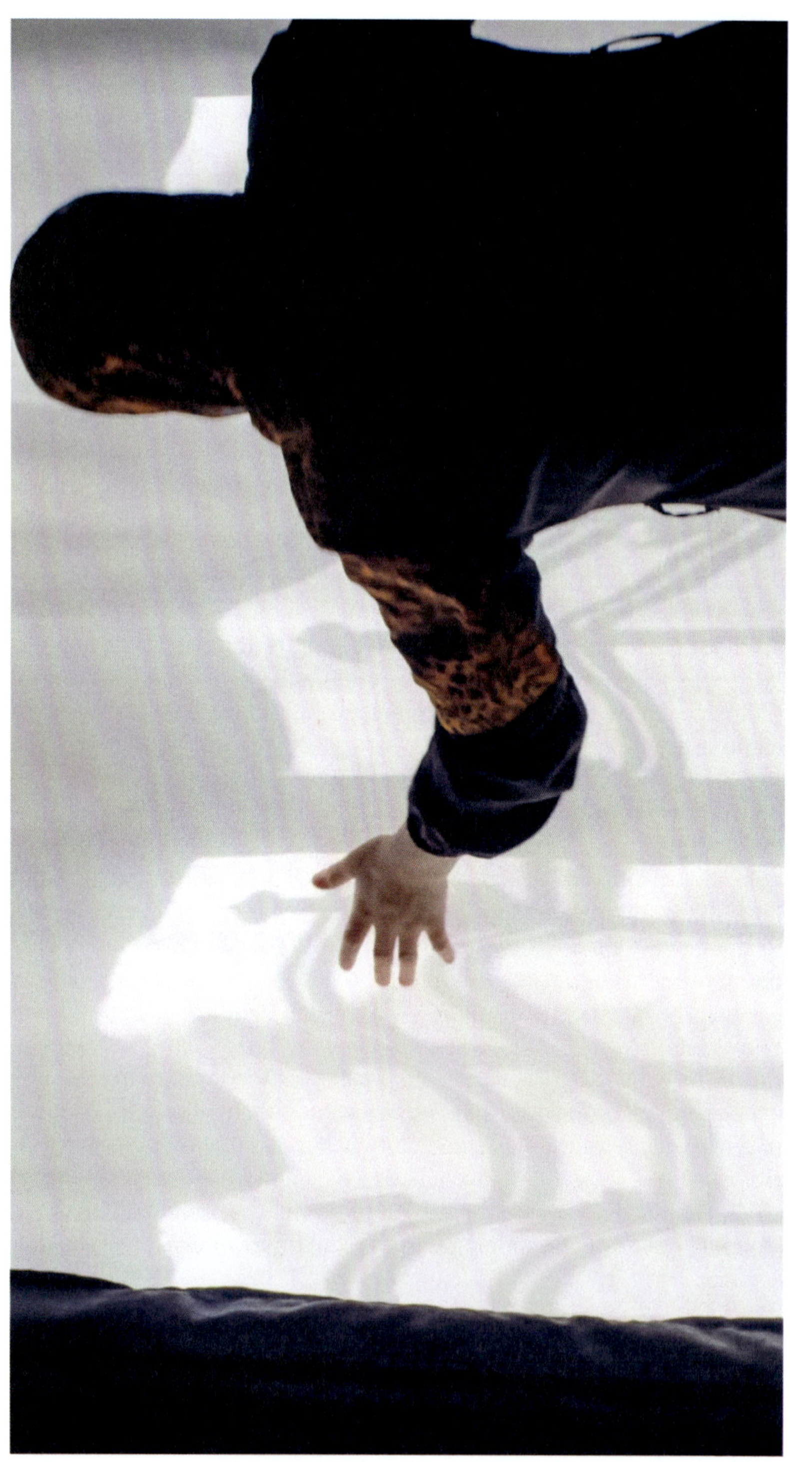

was sometimes difficult, as her situation triggered my own traumatic memories, and I, too, felt the pressure and constriction within my own psyche. In this regard, relationship work lies at the center of my work, both as a filmmaker and as an art therapist.

Tom Kitwood understands personhood as inherently relational—a state of "being in relation."[7] The sense of being a person is not an isolated or fixed quality, but something that is continually nurtured or diminished depending on whether one is valued or de-personalized within a relationship.

As Martin Buber reminds us, "All real living is meeting."[8] It is through such encounters—where the "I" meets a "Thou", opens itself to the other, and allows itself to be moved and transformed—that the self comes into full being. The dialogical, however, extends far beyond verbal communication. It also encompasses nonverbal forms of attunement, resonance, and presence. Communication, in its purest sense, is not merely the exchange of messages but an act of "being-with." In this shared space, connection arises through mutual recognition and an appreciation of the other's uniqueness in the immediacy of the present moment.

Despite the challenges, I felt a strong connection to Iman. Having lived for a long time without contact with other people, and being stigmatized in her small village as the "crazy woman," she had an immense need for human connection free from judgement. It felt natural for the entire crew to offer her the closeness that was important to her. My primary guiding principle throughout the process was to convince both her and the film crew that the most important aspect was to remain in the process, in the here and now, without any expectation that a film must ultimately result.

There were many days when we could not shoot for hours. During these moments, Iman and I would sit in her garden in silence, as it calmed her. Sometimes we picked lemons together, sometimes we sang songs, and sometimes we simply drank coffee. Gradually, I noticed that the heaviness she carried at times gave way to moments of lightness. The more she spoke about her memories at her own pace, the less burdensome they became, and the more space she created for herself, even though it was often painful.

Iman told her story, and we listened, often without the camera, sometimes with it on, though I knew the material was not intended

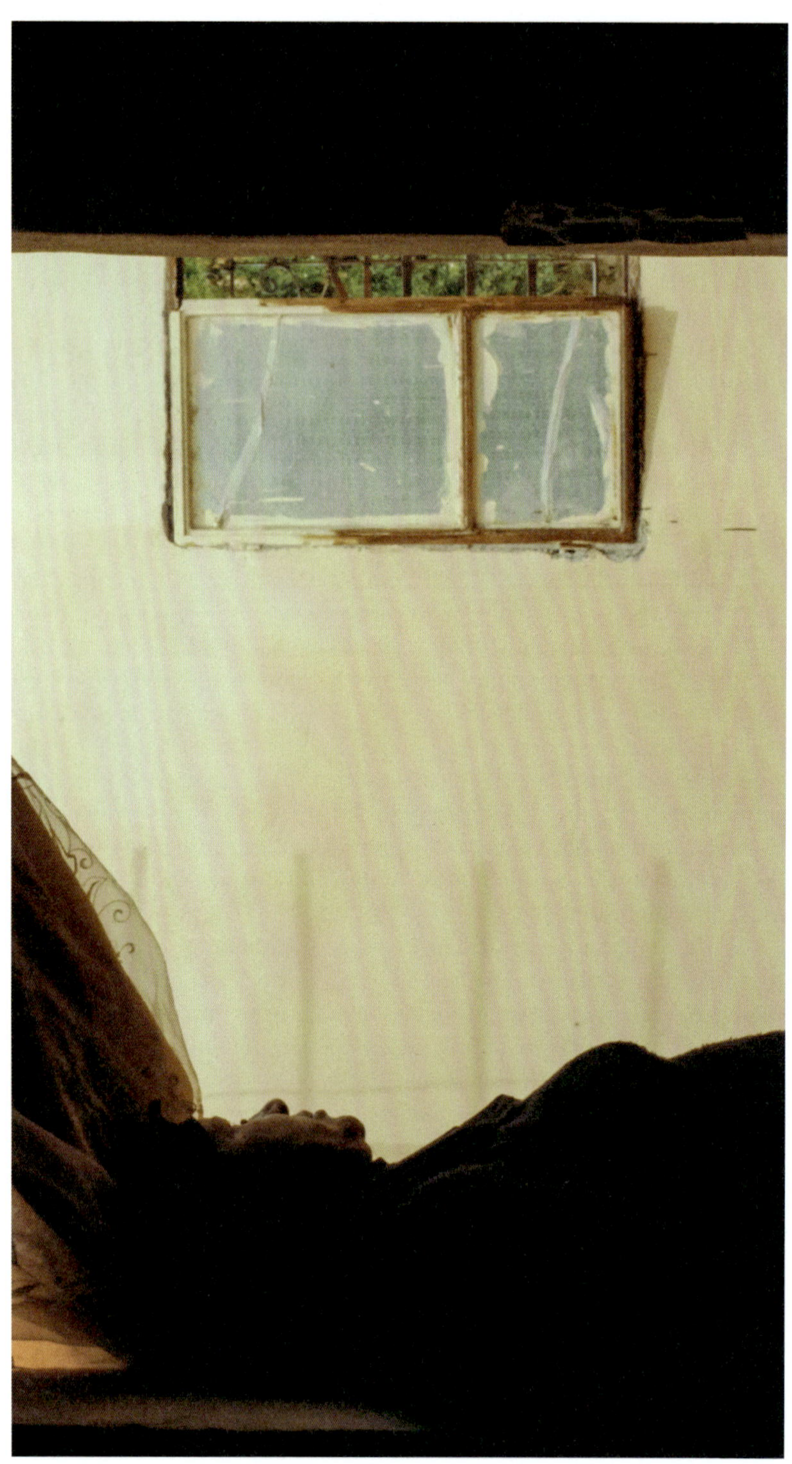

for the film. Speaking about her memories became a relational act; the narrative found an interlocutor who co-shaped it through attention, responses, or gentle opposition.

Within this sometimes nonverbal, liminal space—enriched by compassion and mindfulness—I perceived that the fragile engagement with difficult memories and experiences also held immense transformative potential. A shared narrative space emerged, both verbal and visual, in which Iman could tell her life story and feel fully witnessed.

The processual relationship between filmmaker and protagonist can be understood as an ongoing intersubjective event, in which the central concern is an attunement toward what can be co-created. From this intersubjective connection, "moments of encounter" may crystallize—instances of heightened intensity in which unexpected, transformative experiences emerge. Such moments, often described as "moments of wonder," occur when the ordinary is transcended and the artistic process gives rise to the evocative and the new.

These moments cannot be forced or precisely defined, yet their conditions can be cultivated: by providing time and space, remaining receptive to the unforeseen, respecting one another's symbolism and sense of form, and acknowledging the persistence and extravagance of creative passion.

These conditions simultaneously catalyze transformation within the participants. The possibility of this transformation—whether conceptualized as sublimation or otherwise—is significantly diminished if individuals are not afforded time to think, feel, and become, or if the creative process is not grounded in positive encounters shaped by sensory perception, trust, and mutual modification.

During the shooting of *ANQA*, there were moments when we needed to wait for a long time, sometimes hours, until Iman had the mental space and emotional calm to begin speaking, to take an action, or simply to engage in a conversation with us. This often complicated our shooting schedule, yet we knew that she needed this time, that it was essential to the process overall. We never regarded this time as lost; on the contrary, we understood that if we waited until Iman was ready, we would arrive at what we needed with something as subtle as the blink of an eye. This shift in thinking allowed us to wait patiently for her, with attentiveness rather than impatience.

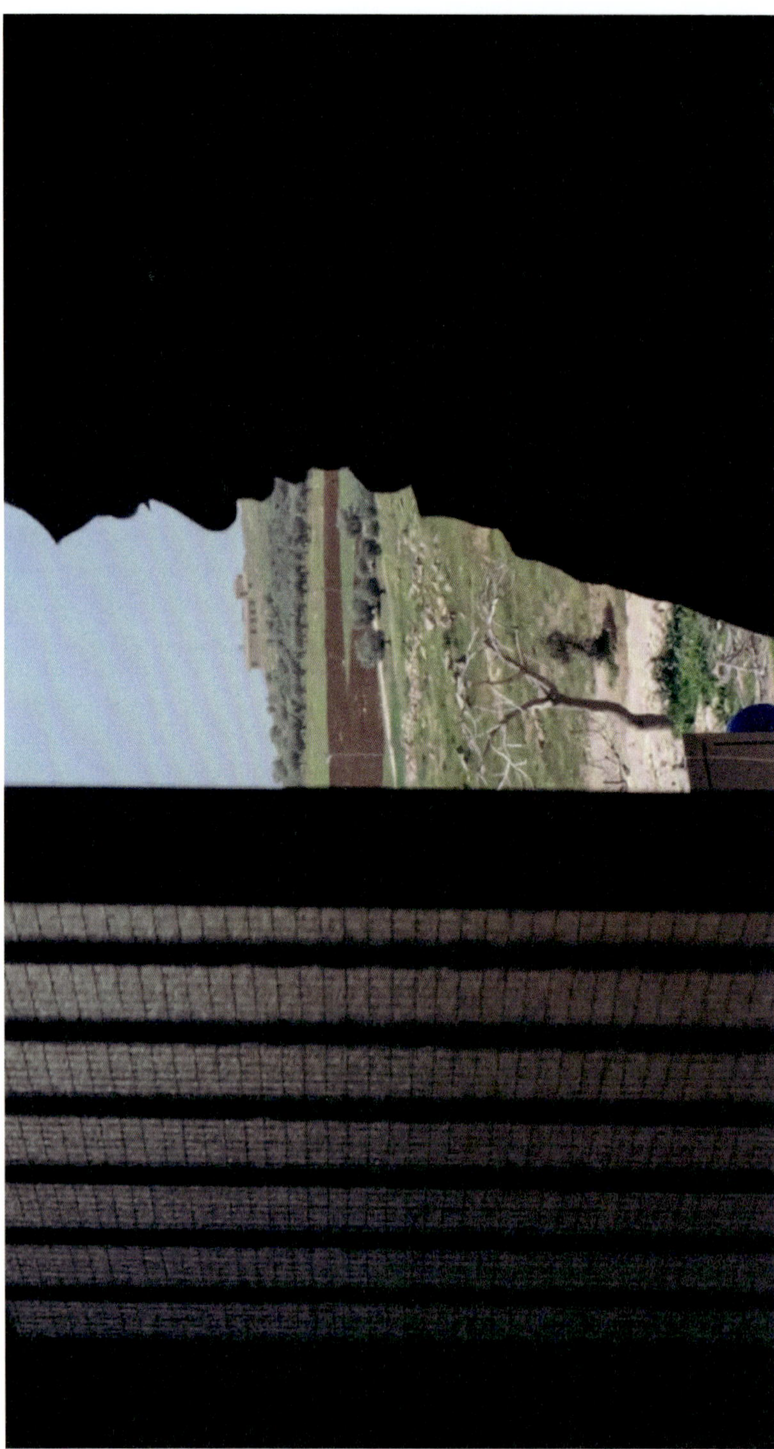

At the same time, Iman was a very fast-moving person. Her actions, whether cleaning, cooking, or moving around the house, were often sudden and restless, as a result of her psychological state. For the filming process, this rhythm required a different kind of negotiation. We needed to speak with her and reach a mutual understanding so that she would occasionally slow down for us to adjust our physical positions, the placement of the camera, or to make other technical preparations.

This dynamic—her need for time to arrive emotionally, our need for time to prepare technically—became a living example of mutual modification. It reflected the reciprocity of our process, where both sides adapted to one another's pace and rhythm. What made this possible was the trust at the foundation of our relationship.

A classical example of such relational dynamics can be observed in the concept of sociable solitude—the state of relaxed tension between mother and child. A child develops the capacity for exploration and imagination when the mother provides safety and trust, allowing the child to play and navigate fantasy under her benevolent but unobtrusive presence. From this emerges a transitional space in which reality and imagination flow together.

The filmmaker–protagonist relationship functions within a similar transitional space. The filmmaker's role should be to accompany and support the protagonist through a working alliance—without imposing ideas or interfering—allowing the participant to immerse themselves in their inner world, explore fantasies, desires, fears, and hopes, and express these through images. This space, where the participant's inner life is honored and agency is fostered, enables the protagonist to both witness and be witnessed, facilitating a positive reconstruction of experience.

The act of giving protagonists the opportunity to tell their own stories transforms both the filmmaker and the film itself into witnesses of personal history. The filmmaking process thus becomes a relational act of testimony, in which the subjects are invited not merely to recount but to *re-author* their lived experiences. This re-authoring functions as a form of narrative repair, allowing the protagonist to reconfigure fragmented or painful memories through symbolic play within the filmic environment. As trauma theorists such as Judith Herman and Dori Laub suggest, the act of bearing witness within a safe and empathic

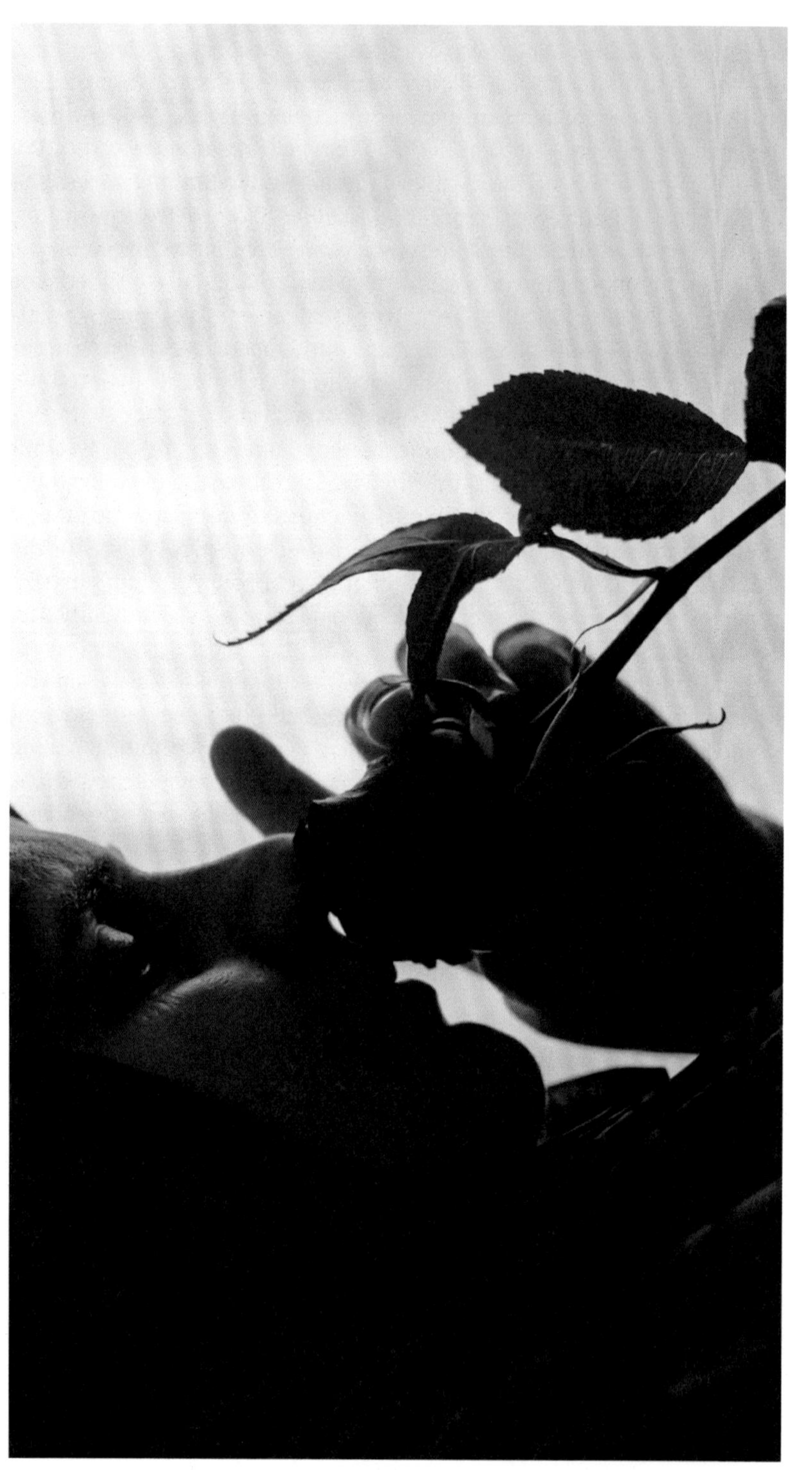

framework enables survivors to integrate traumatic experiences into coherent narratives, thereby facilitating psychic healing.[9]

I often gave Iman an analog camera to carry with her, for her to film whenever she wished. This allowed me to understand how she perceived the world around her, what captured her attention, and where I could "dock" when verbal communication was difficult. In other words, with the help of images I could link up with her world when verbal communication was not possible. Sometimes, when words failed, she expressed her memories as imaginative images and metaphors, transforming violent or painful experiences into narratively and visually accessible forms.

The filmic space, while rooted in the gravity of lived experience, simultaneously retains a dimension of playfulness. Echoing Winnicott's concept of the potential space, this environment allows for experimentation, improvisation, and the imaginative reworking of self-narratives. Within this intersection of play and testimony, the boundaries between memory, fiction, and creation blur, opening a psychological and aesthetic zone, where personal histories can be both revisited and transformed.

Consequently, the filmic act of witnessing extends beyond documentation—it becomes a participatory process of mutual becoming, grounded in intersubjective dynamics. In this sense, the cinematic encounter engages deeply with the themes of personal (hi)story, memory, and witnessing. The film not only records but *rewrites*; it embodies the elasticity of memory as it moves between recollection and re-imagination. The protagonists' stories evolve within this space of shared authorship, where remembering is both an act of survival and an act of creation. Through this process, the camera assumes the role of an ethical companion—observing, listening, and holding the fragile balance between pain and play, testimony and transformation.

Every human being possesses the faculty of imagination as a transformative, almost magical force. Yet for many, the access to their inner imagery lies buried and must first be uncovered. Such an approach facilitates the awakening of these inner images, inviting them back into consciousness and form. The camera and the materials of filmmaking function as mediators between consciousness and the unconscious—a language that can speak where words may fail.

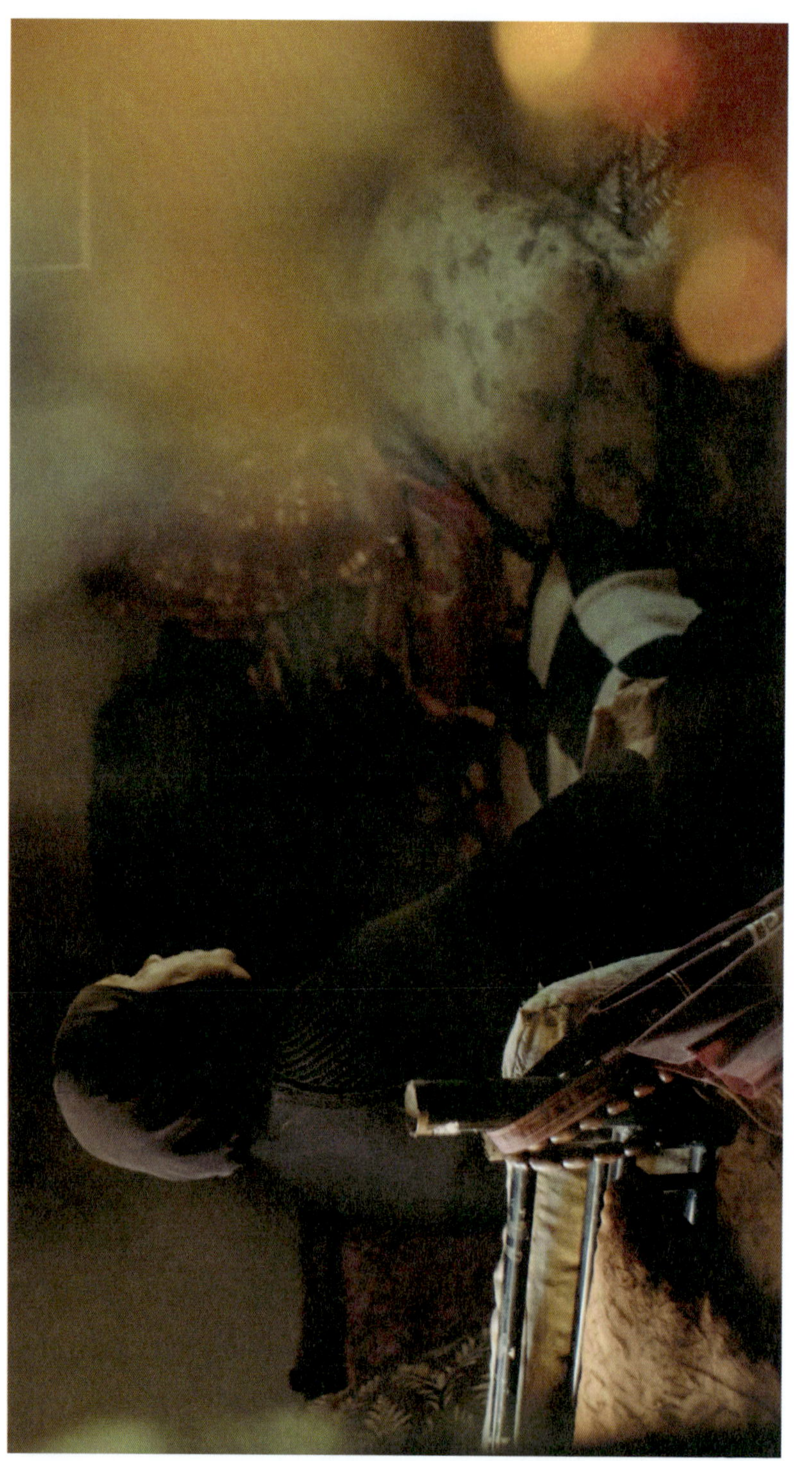

My approach, therefore, is sometimes to cultivate a language of silence—even a linguistic silence—where information is absent, fragmented, or suspended, and to use this shared silent language as a narrative and transformative tool. Silence allows for the opening and closing of spaces where words may not suffice; it becomes a medium through which collective memories are born and new inner images emerge, moving and transforming in resonance with the unconscious. In these "off moments" and "off spaces," where, enriched by gaps in knowledge, truth is interpreted by the audience and politically renegotiated, the cinematic encounter enables alternative forms of narration.

Ultimately, the process of image-making, whether within therapy or film, can be understood as a practice of restoring access to the inner language of a person. It is a way of giving form to what has been repressed, forgotten, or fragmented—transforming internal imagery into visible and shareable expression. This process gives rise to an experience of continuity and coherence. The potent and embodied nature of the creative act functions as a catalyst for reactivating existing memory images, bringing them into the present, transforming them, and generating new ones. Through this dynamic interplay of memory and imagination, the creative process animates the dormant layers of personal history, allowing past experiences to be re-experienced, reshaped, and integrated through artistic expression.

Although the terms "memory" and "remembering" are often used synonymously, they differ in essential ways. Memory refers to a structure or process—a neural and cognitive system—whereas remembering is an active process, a performative act. Memory may be understood as a form of storage, while remembering is a cognitive-psychological construction that must first become conscious before it can be articulated in language. Memory relates to the past, while remembering reconstructs that past through perception in the present moment. Memory occupies a fixed position, whereas remembering is perspectival and fluid, continually reshaping experience as it is recalled and retold.

Whenever we remember a past experience, we do not access something stored in the brain. Rather, we construct an entirely new experience through an imaginative process. Although this act of construction draws upon traces of the original event, that event itself has irrevocably disappeared; what exists in the present moment is our imagination.

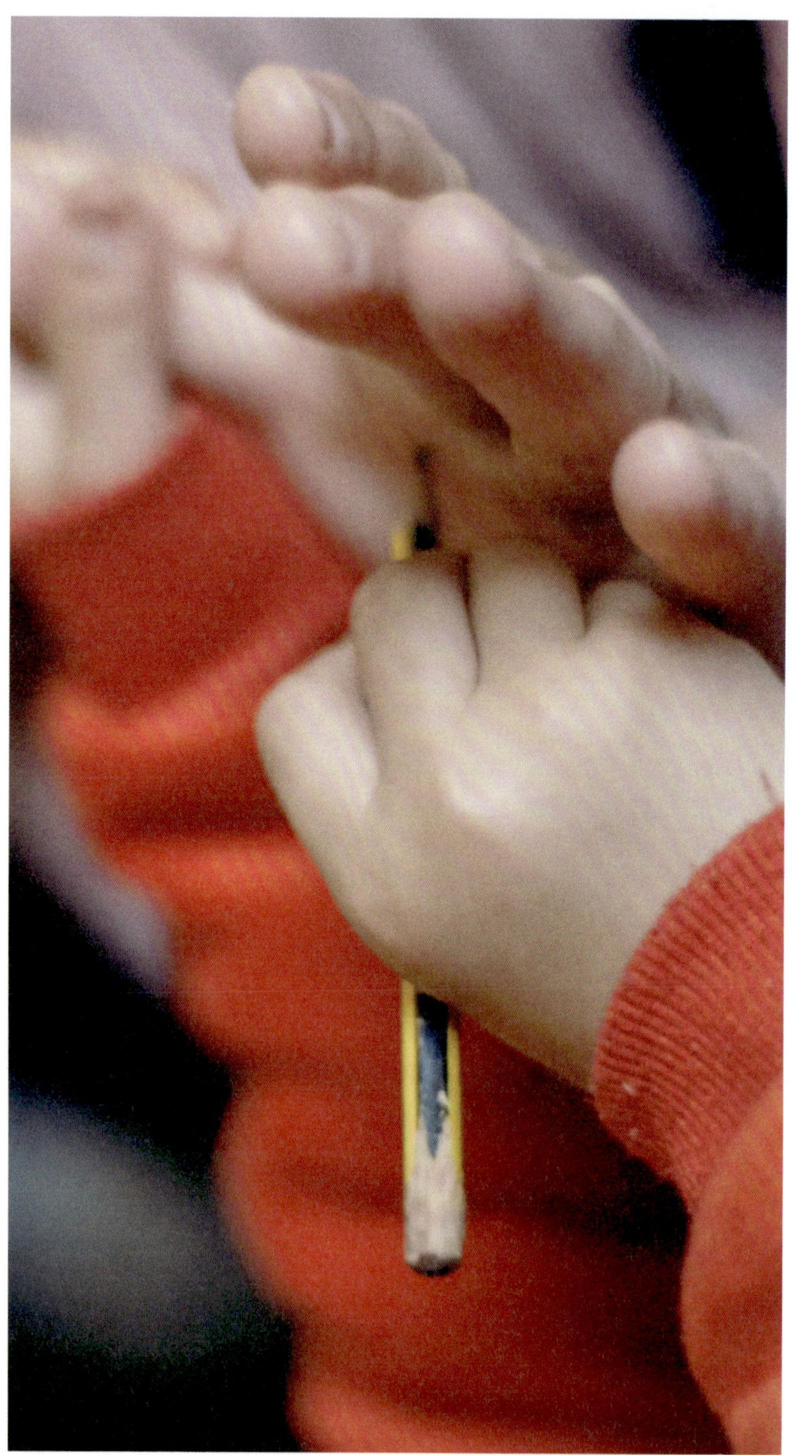

The power of imagination allows us to move beyond what has actually happened or is happening. Each act of remembering is an act of re-creation. This process of reconstruction is not a mere imitation of what once occurred, but a transformative re-formation, a renewal, performed with the imagination. Through the act of narrating memory, a person weaves together the information stored within the memory system—the remembered—with elements of fiction. In the process of remembering, gaps in memory can be completed or bridged through imaginative reconstruction.

Both terms, remembering and narration, describe ways in which an individual—or a community—constructs a version of the past within the present, often with the aim of shaping a desired future. Remembering is thus a spontaneous form of creativity, an expression of the psyche's freedom and its capacity to shape and give form to experience. It unfolds in this present moment, within the "intermediate space," where past and present, reality and imagination, converge.

Remembering and storytelling together shape a coherent sense of self. Storytelling is an inherently relational act. Memories endure most when shared, as recollection reshapes them into stories, into inner images and narrated images.

This is precisely where the filmmaking process takes on a profound psychological and symbolic significance. I perceive deep parallels between the act of remembering and the act of cinematic creation—both involve the reconstruction of fragments, the weaving of lived experience into meaningful narrative, and the transformation of psychic material into images. Just as recollection brings unconscious or partially repressed contents into consciousness, filmmaking gathers experiences, memories, and sensations, allowing them to emerge as symbolic, imagistic, and narratively structured forms. It is within this dynamic interplay between memory and imagination, past and present, that the process of individuation subtly unfolds.

In this light, film becomes not merely a medium of representation but a transitional, liminal space—a potential space, in Winnicottian terms—where both filmmaker and protagonist engage in a relational and intersubjective encounter. The cinematic field functions as a container for unconscious material, allowing images, fantasies, and archetypal motifs to surface, interact, and crystallize into visual form.

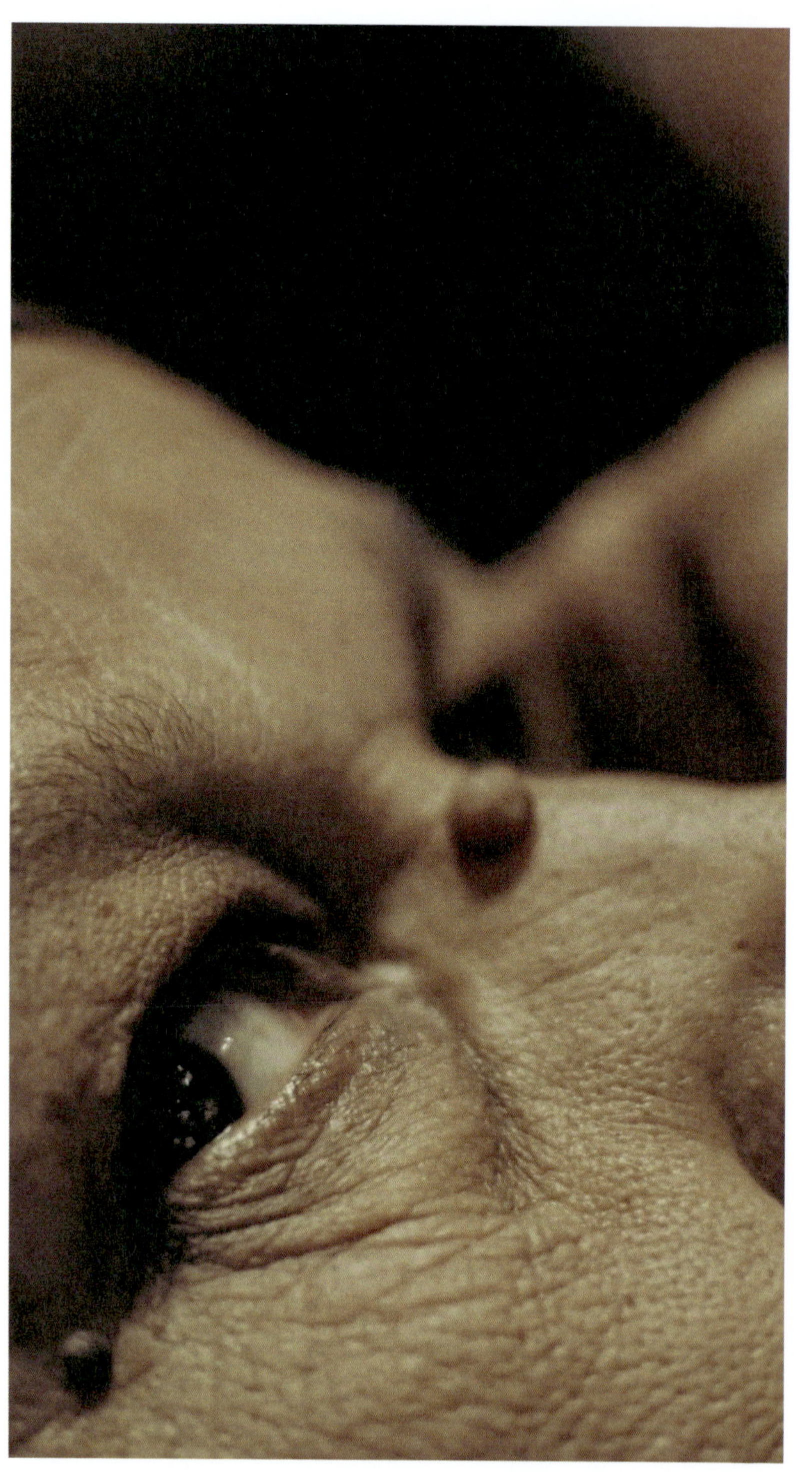

The creative and relational dimensions of this practice allow for a kind of co-individuation: the protagonist discovers new forms of self-expression and agency, while the filmmaker's own psychic and aesthetic sensibilities are simultaneously engaged and expanded. The shared symbolic space of film is both a mirror and a vessel for the psyche—a medium in which the inner life is rendered tangible, and where the work of remembering and creating can converge toward psychological wholeness.

Within our relational narrative space, made possible through the mindful attention of the entire crew of *ANQA*, Iman often experienced moments that allowed her to move from constriction, rigidity, and shame toward lightness, playfulness, and motion. The act of creating images brought a dynamic, fluid, and playful quality to her life story. Her memories and dreams were transformed into images that entered the film in various forms. My images and hers intertwined, creating the film's visual universe. Iman was able to move beyond the literal events of her past, to experience a release from painful memories, a new encounter with life, a transformation that manifested in the closing sentence of the film: "I exist."

1 This argument resonates with Trinh T. Minh-ha's critique of documentary representation; see *When the Moon Waxes Red: Representation, Gender and Cultural Politics* (New York, 1991), where she problematizes the politics of the cinematic gaze and the production of otherness.

2 "In haptic visuality, the eyes themselves function like organs of touch." Laura U. Marks, *The Skin of the Film: Intercultural Cinema, Embodiment, and the Senses* (Durham, 2000), p. 162.

3 The notion of a "right to the dignified image" is discussed in John Fox and The Abounaddara Film Collective, "Representational Regimes: A Conversation with Abounaddara," *World Records Journal* (2017), https://worldrecordsjournal.org/representational-regimes-a-conversation-with-abounaddara/, accessed May 14, 2026.

4 Donald W. Winnicott, *Playing and Reality* (London, 1971), p. 146.

5 Judith Lewis Herman, *Trauma and Recovery: The Aftermath of Violence—From Domestic Abuse to Political Terror* (New York, 1992).

6 Jessica Benjamin, *Like Subjects, Love Objects: Essays on Recognition and Sexual Difference* (New Haven, 1995), p. 16.

7 Tom Kitwood, "On Being a Person," in *Dementia Reconsidered: The Person Comes First* (Buckingham, 1997), pp. 7–19.

8 Martin Buber, *I and Thou*, trans. Ronald Gregor Smith (Edinburgh, 1997), p. 11.

9 Dori Laub, "Truth and Testimony: The Process and the Struggle," in *Trauma: Explorations in Memory*, ed. Cathy Caruth (Baltimore, 1995), pp. 61–75.

Fiction as a Document Vol. 1: Soldiers. Story from Ferentari
Ivana Mladenović

In his introduction to the collection *What Now? Presenting Reenactment* (2009), Jonathan Kahana reflects on the difficulty of placing such a wide array of practices under the single umbrella "reenactment." The ubiquity of reenactment—stretching from Hollywood blockbusters to auteur cinema, and forming the backbone of television news and popular culture—makes it a crucial method through which the moving image engages with history, memory, and collective imagination. Kahana challenges the idea of authenticity by posing the question of how it may be defined when reenactment serves a variety of functions and circumstances. He contends that modern reenactment goes beyond this model, encompassing ritual, therapeutic, pedagogical, and self-reflexive practices that engage not only with the past but also with memory, trauma, and repetition, in contrast to early theories that closely linked reenactment to documentary realism and historical fidelity.

As a director of both documentary and fiction films, I discovered that all my work is deeply connected to the practice of reenactment, even if often unconsciously. The films I have made so far are based on real experiences, reconstructed and re-staged together with the protagonists. I encountered this method in Florin Șerban's film *When I Want to Whistle, I Whistle* (2012), which was a basis for my own documentary *Turn off the Lights* (2012), in which working with non-professional actors and real situations was essential. In *Soldiers. Story from Ferentari* (2017), based on the autobiographical novel by Adrian Schiop, the author of the book is also the main actor; he tells the story of his relationship with a former inmate from a marginalized neighborhood in Bucharest, and explores the tensions between the majority and the

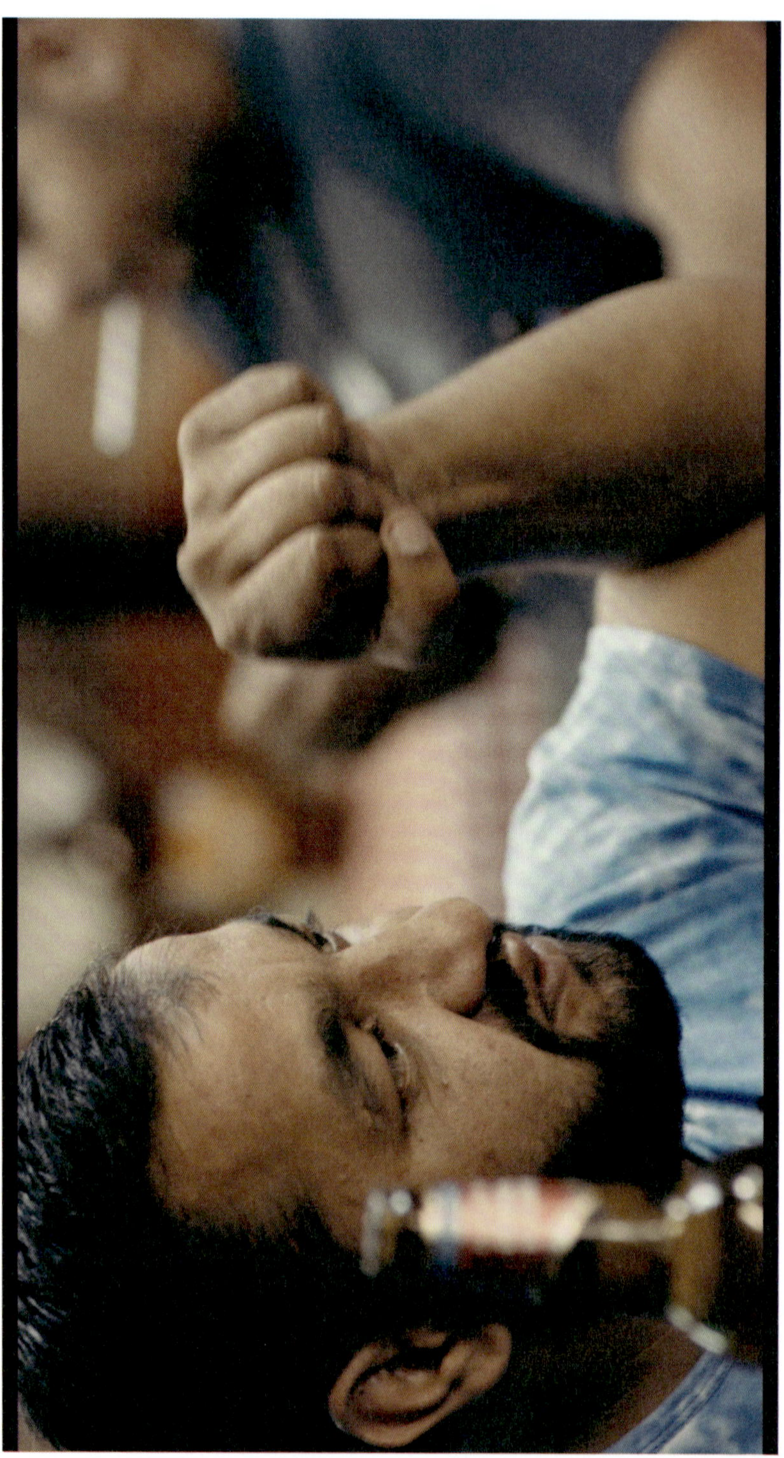

Roma minority. In *Ivana the Terrible* (2019), I used my own personal experience, recreating real events with the people who lived them alongside me. I fictionalized as little as possible so that the film would become almost a fragment of reality.

In *Reenactment as an Event in Contemporary Cinema* (2011), Sylvie Jasen focuses on the nature of reenactment and its specific characteristics within contemporary film. For her, reenactment is not an imitation performed for the screen; rather, reenactment permeates the entire process of filmmaking. In her PhD research, Sylvie Jasen compares various theories of authenticity in reenactment, examining how different scholars approach the search for truth in reconstructed performance, and whether elements such as casting, the use of real locations, or the incorporation of archival material shape the viewer's perception of truth. She begins with Brian Winston's contribution in *Lies, Damn Lies and Documentaries* (2000), where he rejects purist critiques and argues that authenticity resides not in original people or places, but in the plausibility of actions, as exemplified by Humphrey Jennings's *Fires Were Started* (1943), in which real firefighters re-create typical experiences rather than actual historical events. Other scholars, such as Steven Lipkin and Derek Paget, link authenticity more closely to actual participants, locations, and archival materials, while Ivone Margulies highlights the role of the non-professional "social actor" as a conduit through which memory and activism can be sustained and mobilized, underscoring its pedagogical dimension. Vanessa Agnew frames reenactment as an emancipatory practice that enables communities to reclaim history and recover their past; in *Once More ... With Feeling* (2007), Robert Blackson distinguishes reenactment from repetition or simulation, highlighting its openness to improvisation—in reenactment truth arises from the participants' subjective engagement and their capacity to inhabit history on their own terms, rather than from factual accuracy. Jasen extends this conversation through case studies on films that reconstruct trauma, often using amateur actors who portray themselves and revisit personal memories. In this way, the embodied performance of the individual, whose presence acts as a mediator between the historical event and its cinematic reconstruction, becomes inextricably linked to authenticity. My documentary *Turn Off the Lights* (2012) follows the lives of three young ex-convicts

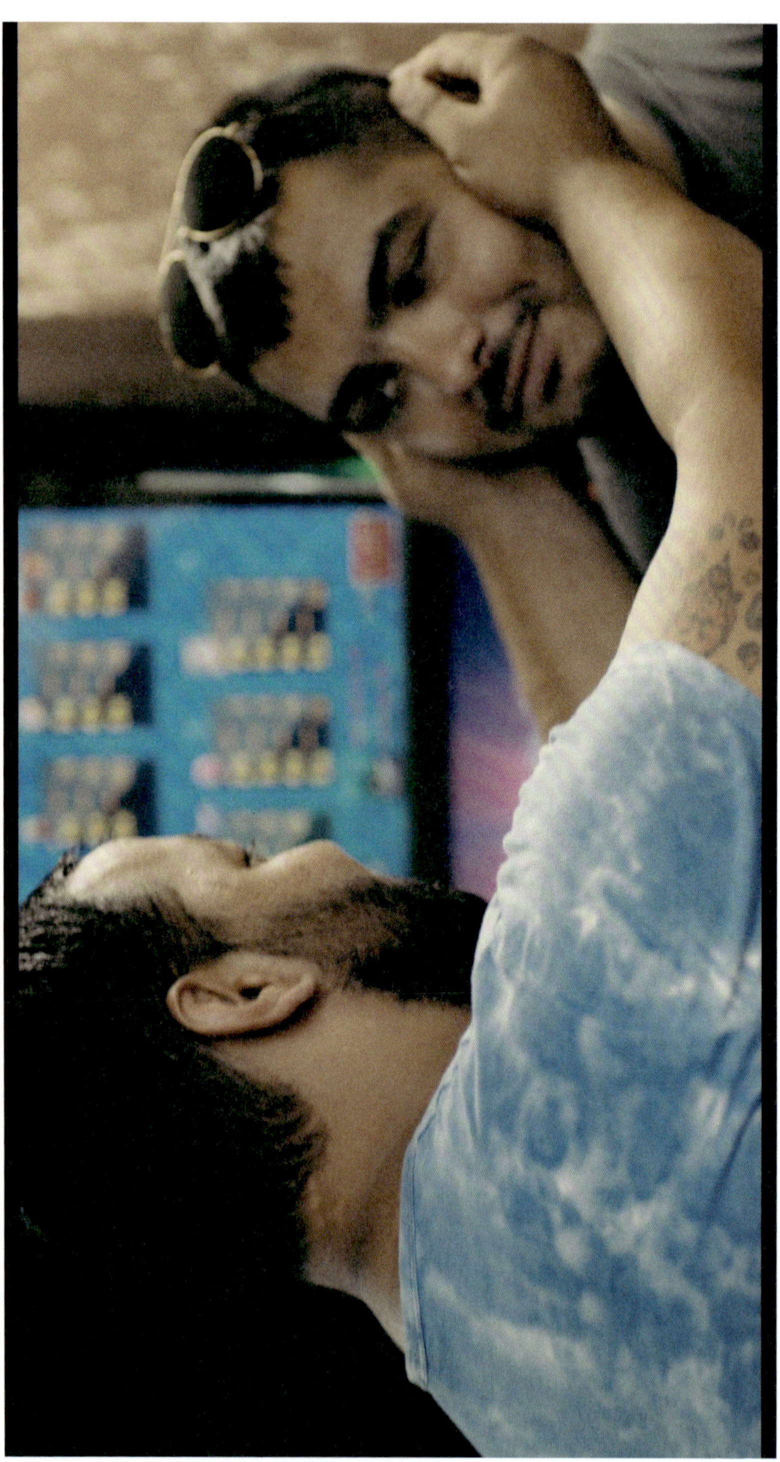

attempting social reintegration. The film is based on an acting workshop that Florin Șerban conducted in Romanian prisons to cast his own film *When I Want to Whistle, I Whistle* (2012). The young men went through a six-month training process, in which they learned acting in order to play roles very close to their real-life experiences and personalities; I then made a film that followed their lives after release. I certainly can't say that the workshops or acting experiences directly influenced how they behaved in my documentary, but there was some kind of impact. I realized that my film, though documentary, could also be seen as deep fiction.

A similar experience of being unable to separate fiction from documentary occurred when I later decided to transform Adrian Schiop's autobiographical book *Soldiers: Story from Ferentari* (2017) into a work of cinematic fiction. The book tells the story of an anthropologist who, as part of his doctoral research, moves into the most deprived part of Bucharest, Ferentari, to study the social milieu of those who listen to and make Roma manele music. Adrian, the author and main character, combines autobiographical elements with field research when he meets Alberto, a man without identity documents who spent 15 years in prison. He offers to help the anthropologist navigate Ferentari and to support him in writing his study on manele music. Their relationship grows into something more complex, encompassing both personal and social tensions. My film, deeply rooted in the book, focuses on the life of the Roma community in Ferentari, a largely Roma neighborhood, and explores the conflicts between social classes and economic dependency, while the love story between the two men acts as the emotional center of the narrative.

My priority, in making the film, was to figure out how this story could be conveyed emotionally, while at the same time depicting the complex relationship between the Romanian majority and the Roma minority. In his book, Schiop does not clearly separate autobiographical testimony from fiction—what mattered was the feeling that it was both. That approach inspired me, and that sense of the "real" suffering of Ferentari was what I wanted to portray in the film. I tried to avoid any kind of stereotype and to present the love story of the main characters honestly, without exoticization or sentimentality. I also wanted to depict the social context—the life, sadness, and energy of the community—as I

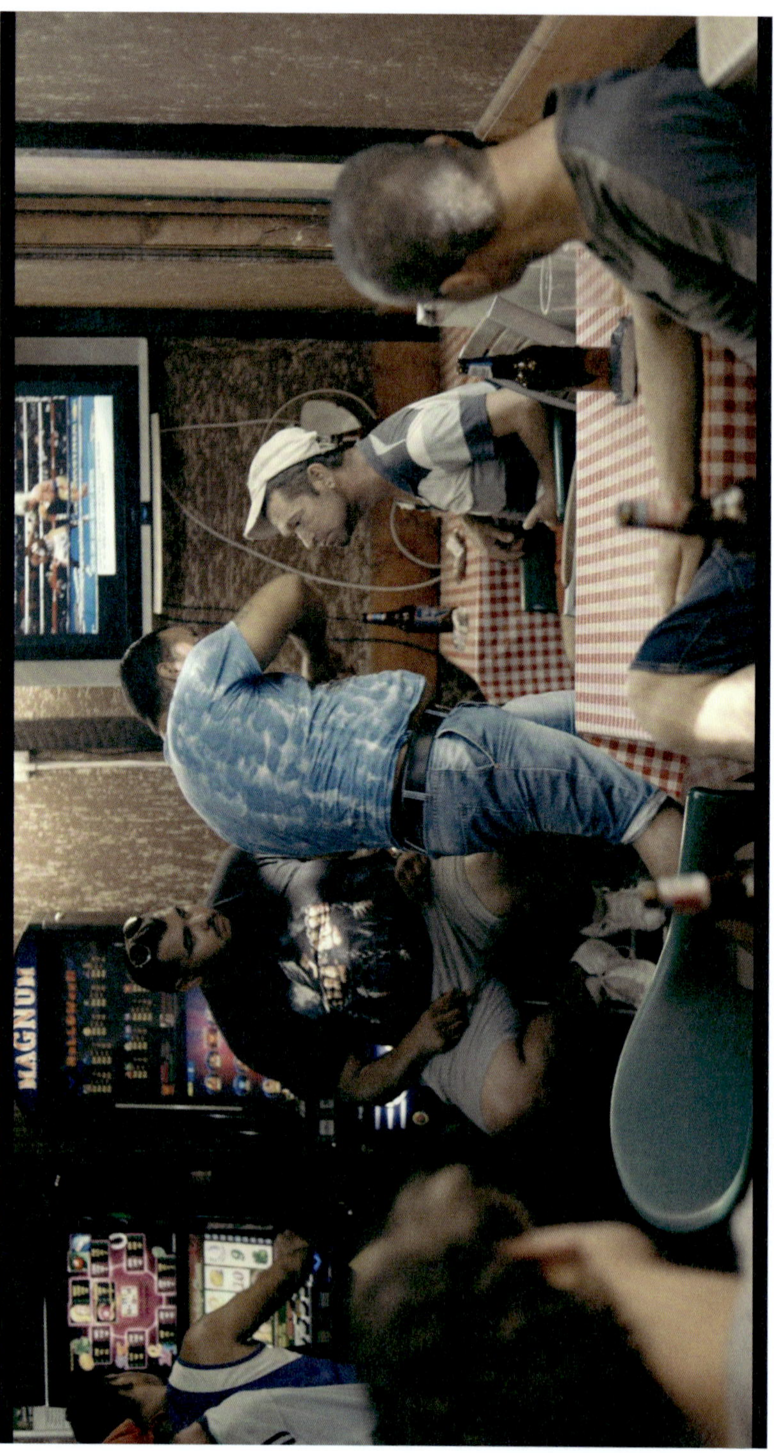
MAGNUM

experienced it myself. My goal was not to make a "faithful copy" of reality but to reveal the truth that emerges only through human contact. The film became, for me, a way to explore both the subject and my own position within that reality.

"Document" became a word that appeared constantly during the film's preparation. At that time, I was collaborating with the ARAS—Romanian Association Against AIDS team (a non-governmental organization running HIV prevention and harm-reduction programs for vulnerable communities), and once a week I joined their mobile medical unit operating in the neighborhood. These visits allowed me to enter the community's everyday life: to observe their relationships, reactions, rhythms. The experience was demanding but crucial to understanding the local context. During this preliminary research and filming stage, I encountered situations that clearly showed how difficult it is to balance documentary fidelity with cinematic structure. The act of filming itself mirrored what the film was about—trust, distrust, boundaries between communities, and invisible power mechanisms that emerge when a camera enters a space to which it doesn't belong.

During the preparations in Ferentari, the atmosphere was tense, and my team and I faced a series of unexpected situations. Residents often used fake names or nicknames when speaking to us, probably out of caution toward outsiders. Even a harmless object, like a rolled-up hard-drive cable the cameraman was carrying, was mistaken for handcuffs, causing suspicion among people in the neighborhood and making them think we might be police or inspectors. These reactions underscored how sensitive the community was to external observers and how complex it is to film authentically in such an environment, something described vividly in Schiop's book. When we set up cameras in certain places, people spontaneously began cleaning the streets and removing trash; the public space suddenly took on a new face. This showed me the interactive relationship between us and the community, and the effect of the presence of the camera on the reality we were trying to capture.

At that time, I wasn't consciously thinking that the film should function as a documentary record, but my decision to shoot in the neighborhood, guided by a mix of rational reflection and an intuitive sense of authenticity, eventually became central to our attempt to present the community and the people living there.

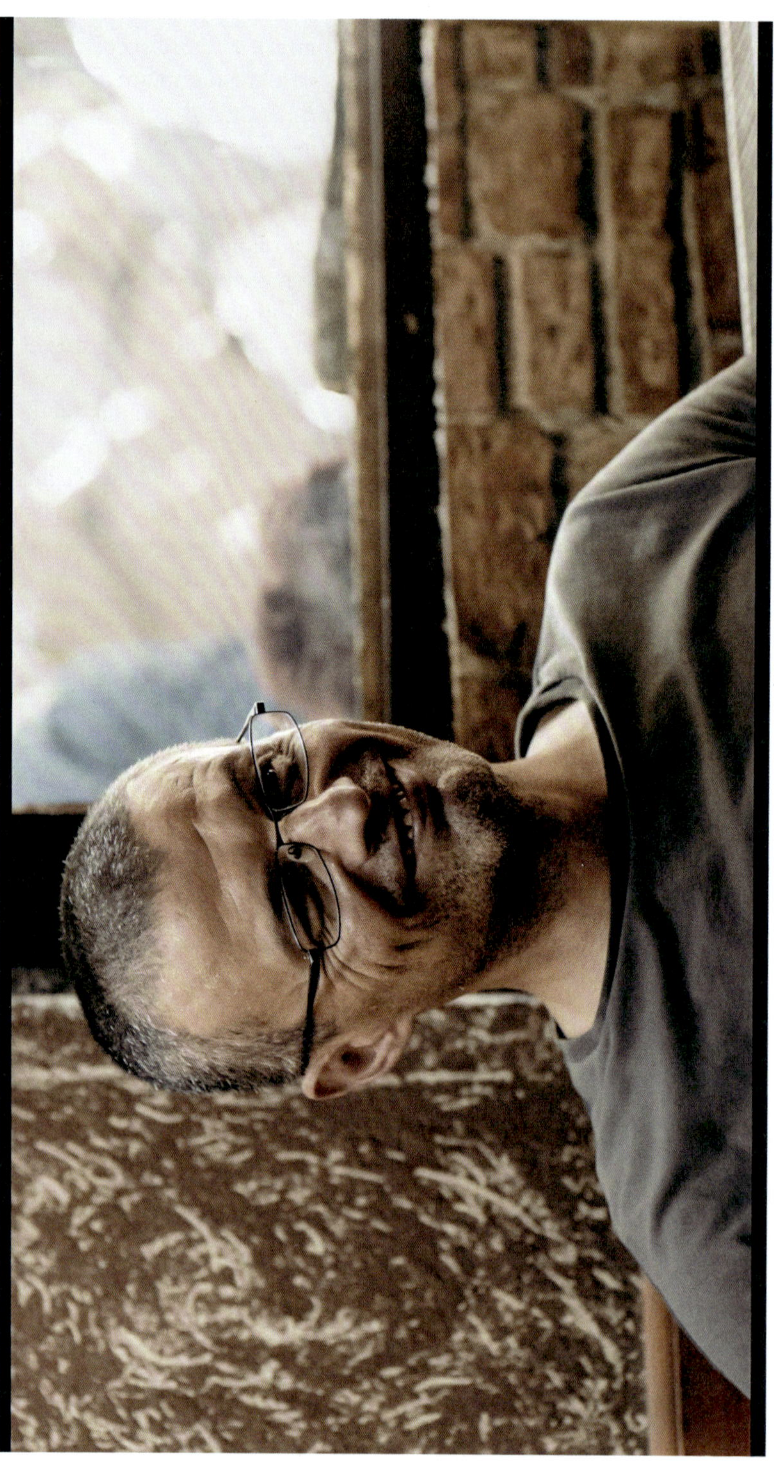

In his essay *Documentary Reenactment and the Fantasmatic Subject* (2008), Bill Nichols, one of the most influential theorists of documentary film, addresses the question of reenactment and its authenticity, and as Jonathan Kahana observes, Nichols is less concerned with reenactment as a straightforward method of authentication but more with its capacity to signal its own construction, to show itself as representation. Every documentary, he argues, contains a "fantasmatic" dimension. When the fantasmatic highlights the gap between the past and the present, it is not a failure of authenticity but a condition of it; only then can reenactment gain both ethical and emotional force, precisely because it reveals what cannot be repeated. The power of documentary is not in reproductions of something that happened, but in the tension between memory and what is lost, what is absent.

When I first read Schiop's book, one of the main questions that arose was who would play the main roles. It was clear that the authenticity of the interpretations of Alberto and Adrian would be crucial for the film. Aware of the way Roma characters had been portrayed in Romanian films and television—often played by a trained actor who does not belong to the community, and caricatured—it was essential to me that the Alberto role be played by someone who truly belonged to the community. I had the feeling—and today I can't say with certainty whether it was methodologically justified—that casting someone "from a higher class who had had more opportunities in life" to play a person from such a marginalized context would create distance and even be insulting.

When it came to production, working with non-professionals involved certain risks, mainly concerning continuity and commitment. There is always a fear that participants might withdraw midway, become unavailable, or struggle with the demands of the role. These concerns are understandable, as people without prior professional experience in film may not always anticipate the intensity and duration of the process. But, having previously worked with non-professional actors, I was aware of that hardship, as well as the unique personal investment when it comes to offering the chance to perform; and when it came to Pavel Vasile Digudai, with whom I had been working on the role for so many months, that uncertainty was worth the risk.

My encounter with Pavel Vasile Digudai, a hospital bodyguard from Ploiești who would play Alberto, happened by chance through mutual

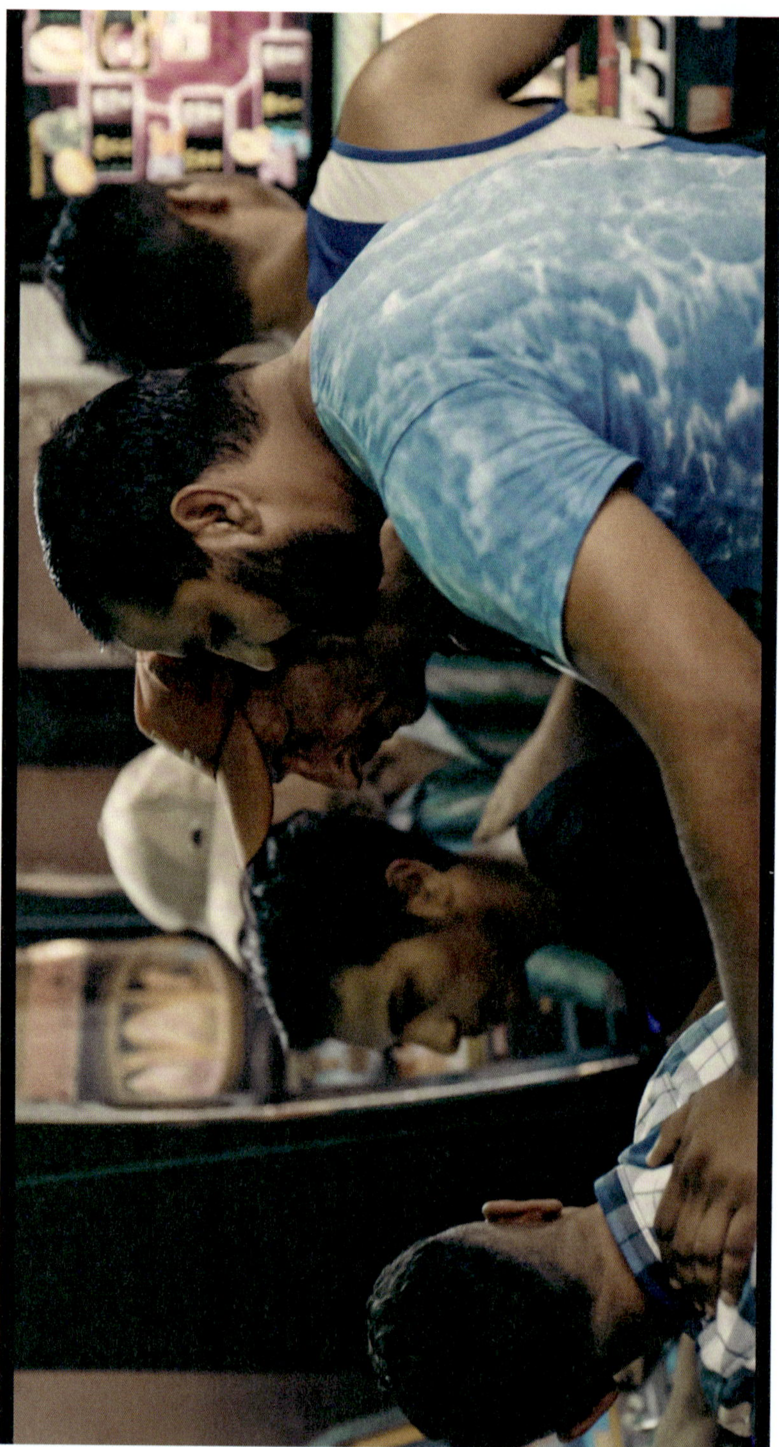

acquaintances. As soon as I saw Digudai, I knew he was the one. He was likable, gentle, with a childlike expression in his eyes. Alberto, in both the book and my film, is conflicted, sometimes rough, but underneath there's immense vulnerability. The process was long and exhausting—we rehearsed for almost a year and a half—and at the same time, I continued casting for the role of Adi, another role that carried enormous weight. Many actors immediately refused; they didn't want to play a homosexual character who begins a relationship with a man from a marginalized community, and even less to act opposite a non-professional. Famous actors would come for the casting and say, "Find me another actor partner, and I'll play it." They saw Digudai as dangerous, too "wild." The role of Adi (Adrian Schiop) required someone who sincerely loved and researched Roma manele music and was genuinely interested in Alberto's life, not someone who distanced himself from the start. In Romanian society there's a huge stigma against manele music—it's all but banned on national radio. Around the time I was preparing the film, 2014–2016, the idea that someone seriously listened to and studied it academically seemed absurd to most actors. When I told them they'd play a PhD student genuinely fascinated by that music, they rolled their eyes, refused, and treated it all as parody.

Finally, I offered the role to Adrian Schiop, the writer himself. Since he was also the film's co-screenwriter, Adrian was spending a lot of time with me and was often present during the preproduction. Naturally, he met Digudai, and their acquaintance quickly grew into a real friendship. Adi was genuinely interested in Digudai, his past, his lifestyle, his thoughts. Throughout the casting process, we often worked with the scene in which Alberto massages Adi. That scene contains the entire dynamic of their relationship: friendship and genuine curiosity for one another, alongside an underlying economic dependence that shapes their interactions. Adi knew the script by heart, so I asked him to play that scene with Digudai, and when I saw them together, I knew that that was the feeling the film needed. Adi initially refused, but after a few months came back and said, "Let's try again."

It often happened that Digudai and Adi gave the same answer when journalists asked them why they decided to make this film: because of money. For Adi, this was likely the primary motivation, though he was also deeply invested in the project and became one of my strongest

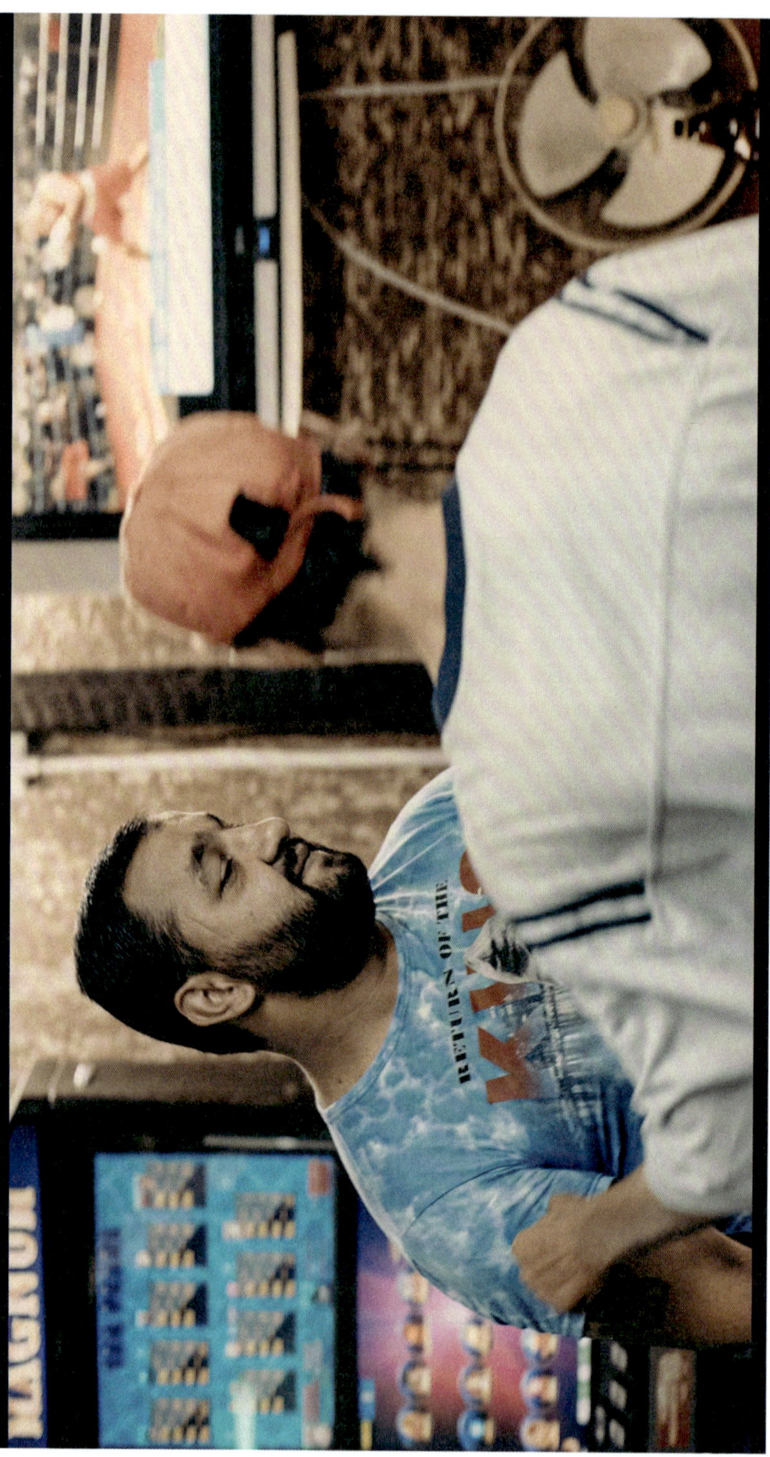
MAGNUM
RETURN OF THE

sources of support. For Digudai, however, the motivation seemed different. I was convinced that he genuinely loved acting, and that the process itself gave him pleasure and a sense of purpose. But since he played a gay character in a country where homophobia is still strong, it was easier for him to say publicly that he did it for money, as a kind of protection. Money was also at the core of both the book and the film. The question of where love and money intersect, and how emotions are shaped by economic circumstances, formed the central thread of the story. Both Adi, who now lives in Ferentari, and Digudai, through their own personal histories and economic positions, seemed to describe the lives of their characters. Again, the conditions of the film's production mirrored the themes of the script itself.

Another major production challenge was my insistence to film in Ferentari. The title, *Soldiers. Story from Ferentari,* made it unacceptable for me to "fake" the whole neighborhood elsewhere, as production initially proposed, arguing that the neighborhood is too dangerous. Their stance was that the area could be reconstructed, "faked" in another Bucharest neighborhood. Such a compromise felt impossible to me, so we rented an apartment in Ferentari, which also became our rehearsal space and the setting for much of the film. This allowed the actors to remain immersed in the neighborhood and for the production team to get to know the reality we were portraying.

Mădălina Botoran, a social worker and psychologist who has long worked with families in Ferentari, was a key contributor to the project. She managed the relationship with the community, making sure it was always based on mutual respect, care, and trust, and kept in regular contact with local families through her professional role. She and the film team both appreciated maintaining polite, courteous, and open lines of contact between the residents and the crew. In addition to her continuous humanitarian activity, Mădălina played a crucial role in the casting process and the choice of Ferentari filming settings/locations.

The casting process for supporting roles was spontaneous and also involved people from the neighborhood: some were reserved, others refused at first, but later returned. The film was created in close collaboration with the community itself: the way the actors were chosen, the way the scenes were improvised, and the constant blurring of the boundaries between documentary and fiction allowed the entire project

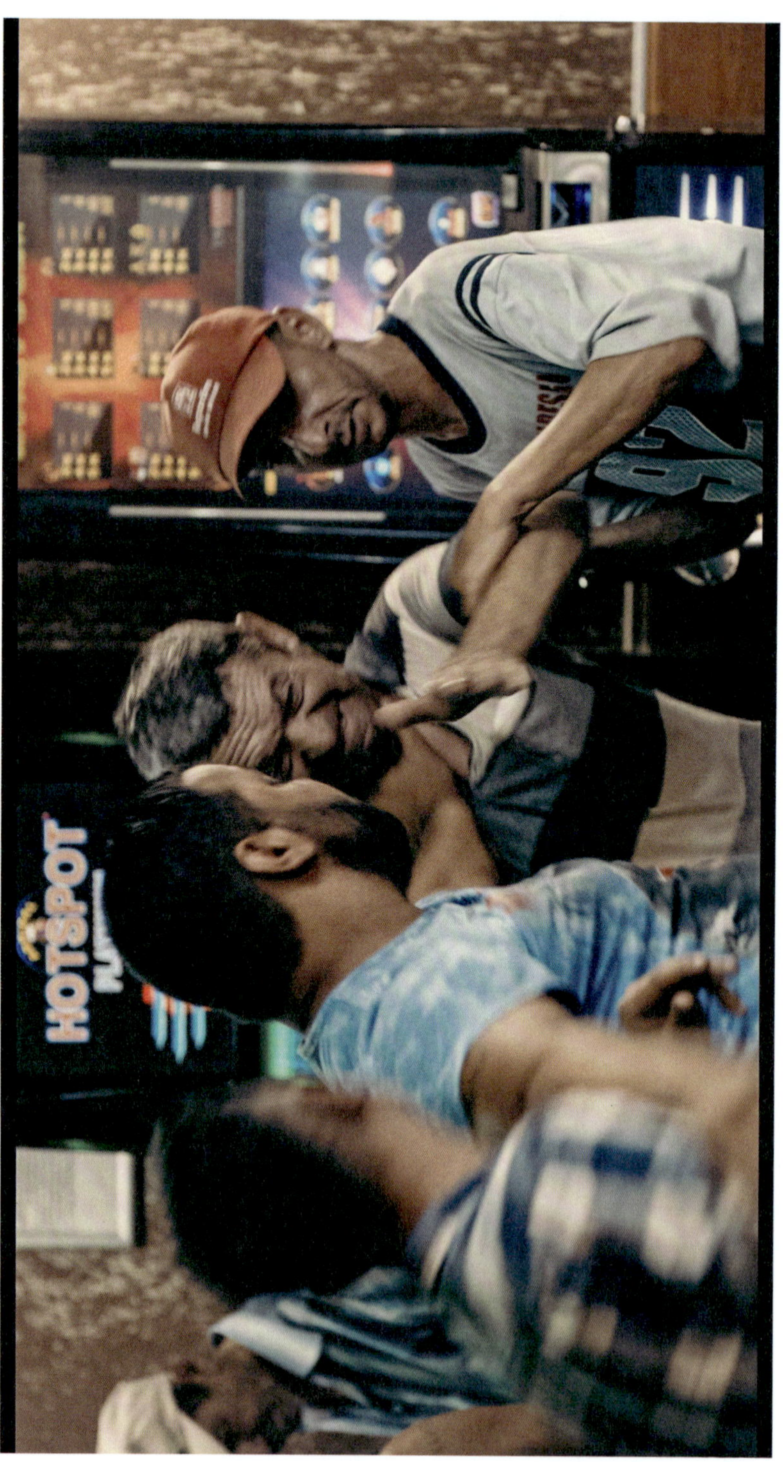
HOTSPOT

to function as a continuous reenactment. Two weeks into the process, we filmed a scene on an actual bus line running through Ferentari. The process was so natural that at some point I lost track of who was an actor, who was an extra, and who was simply a passerby—the experience was confusing.

As Nichols points out, reenactment is not only about reproducing past events but also about social dramaturgy, about how people perform their identities in the presence of the camera. The neighborhood's residents, when acting, were at the same time playing themselves, affirming their own presence and subjectivity in a space—Romanian cinema—that usually excludes them from representation. Even moments of refusal or negotiation become part of that dynamic of reenactment, like when people would ask us to pay to photograph a building or a tree. These are micro-performances of autonomy: the residents refuse to be "objects" of documentation, instead becoming agents who determine their own conditions of visibility. In this sense, the film not only records reality but also reveals real power relations, negotiations, and boundaries that shape how authenticity can be represented.

Two sequences were particularly formative for the film. During preproduction, I visited Dan Bursuc, one of the most influential producers in the manele scene. I went with the producer to see Bursuc at his home, which also functioned as a school for young Roma singers, *Academia de Manele Dan Bursuc,* who lived and trained with him there. I wanted to invite him to play one of the main roles, as Adrian's PhD research around which the film was based (*Șmecherie și lume rea. Universul social al manelelor* by Adrian Schiop) was specifically an ethnographic study of the social context of manele music.

During our first meeting, Bursuc reacted strongly to the idea of a "white" researcher writing about manele, insisting that only someone from within the community could legitimately speak about this music. His response was confrontational and assertive, grounded in claims of lived authority and expertise. Only after I clarified that the film was not an academic study of manele, but a fictional narrative about a character researching it, did he agree to participate. During filming, Bursuc refused to memorize lines and chose to improvise, a condition I accepted in order to preserve the specificity of his voice and self-representation. In the film, the scene with Bursuc reenacted our initial encounter, but

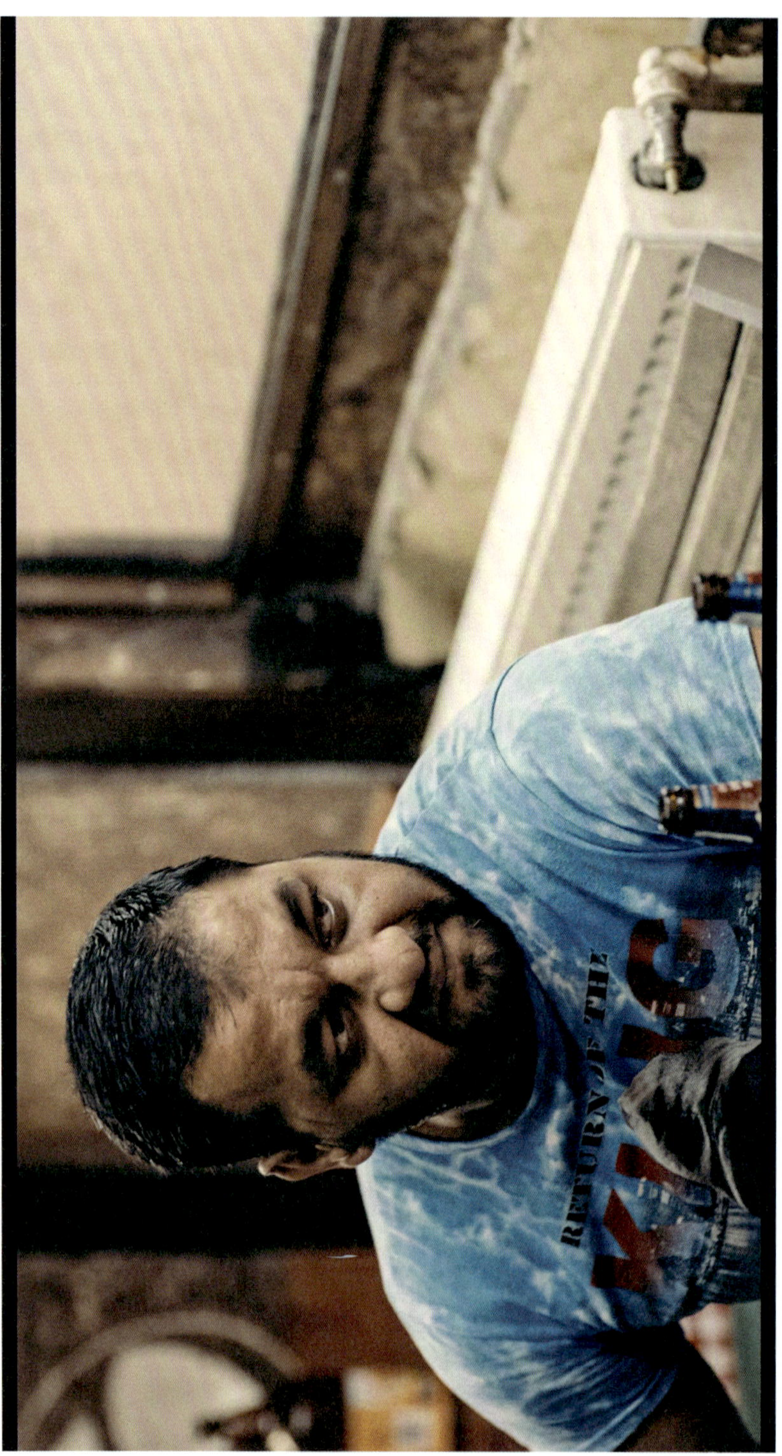

with Adi, instead of myself and the producer, attempting to meet Bursuc and conduct an interview. By staging his initial refusal and assertion of authority, Bursuc unknowingly reaffirmed the same structures of power, dependency, and legitimacy that the film seeks to critically examine.

At the time, Bursuc was running the school for around fifteen young male artists from largely underprivileged backgrounds. One of these young artists, Bulgăraș Nicolae, became part of the scene at Bursuc's insistence. His story of having lived on the streets before being taken in and trained by Bursuc, along with improvised performances by other young singers, emerged organically during filming—these were moments drawn from experience, now reactivated within a fictional framework. Although the scene was formally staged, its content was generated by the participants themselves. As such, it became a hybrid of fiction and lived reality.

Another example of hybrid fiction and lived reality occurred in the Zeicani tavern, where key moments from the book had originally taken place and where we filmed several scenes. Although we were only given permission to shoot in an empty corner of the tavern, without regular guests present, our aim was to reenact the atmosphere and interactions described in the book. The scene recreated Adi's first meeting with Alberto, in which one of Alberto's acquaintances warns Adi about the risks of being involved with Alberto. It was performed by the real Adi, Digudai as Alberto, and a local patron. The actor initially cast for the role, a non-professional from the neighborhood with whom I had worked for over a month, quit on the very day the scene was scheduled to be filmed. With no time to recast, my casting director and I spontaneously invited a passerby outside the tavern to take part in the scene. What followed was a remarkable coincidence: the passerby turned out to be an acquaintance of the real Alberto and had been present when Adi first met him in real life. Although he did not immediately recognize Adi, and although Alberto's real name had been changed in both the book and the script, as the dialogue unfolded, he began to recall the original encounter and responded with lines strikingly close to those written in the script, which he had never seen. At moments, he even referred to Alberto by his real name, rather than the fictional one used in the film. This improvisation, which started out as a practical solution to an unforeseen circumstance, produced a scene that was even closer

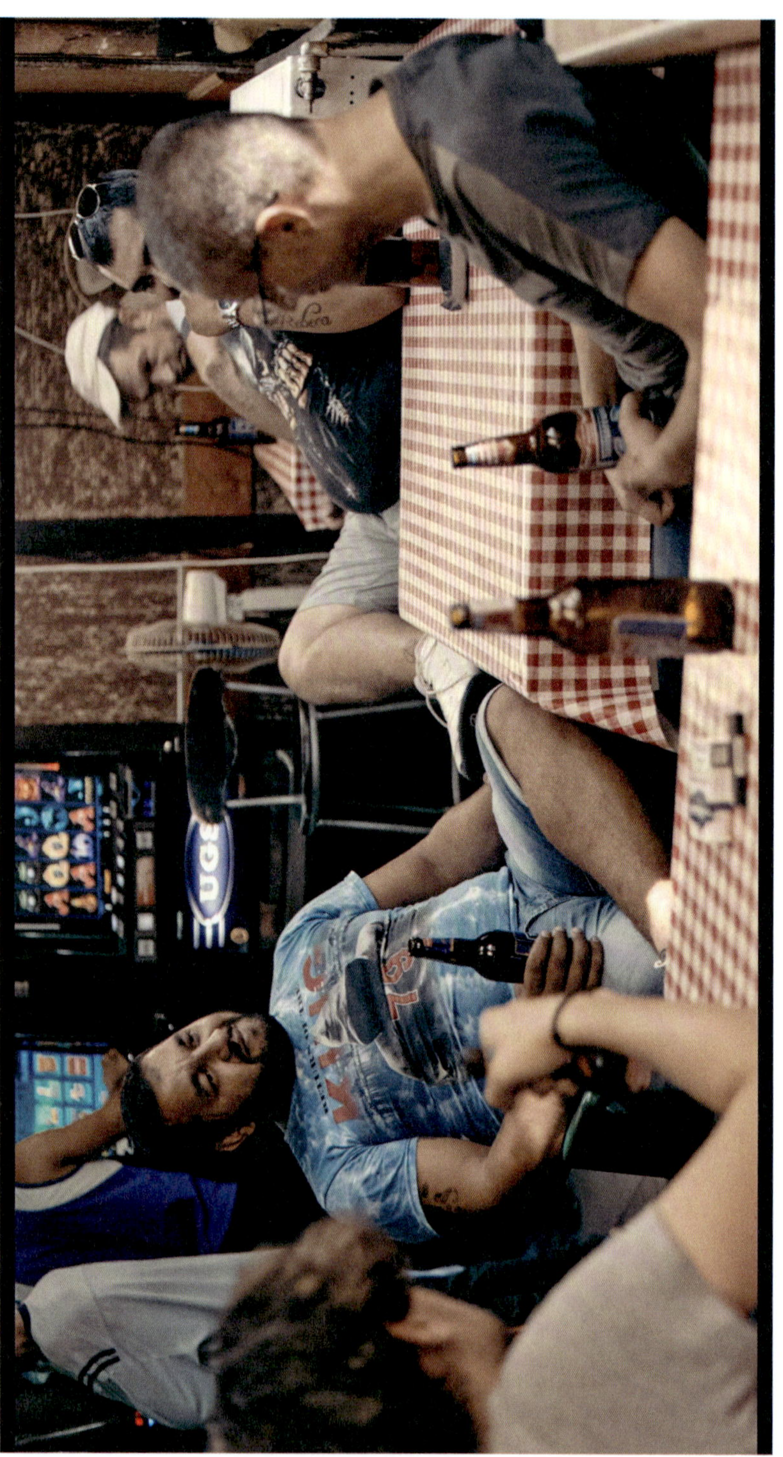

to the initial encounter, even more "authentic" than what we had originally planned—giving up control, and using uncertainty as a technique, created a space where the past and present briefly overlapped.

Personal as social

While *Soldiers. Story from Ferentari* (2017) and *Ivana the Terrible* (2019) both rely on reenactment as a structuring principle, they differ in their approach to authenticity and the degree of self-exposure. In *Soldiers* the reenactment operates within a social framework: it reconstructs a lived experience derived from the autobiographical novel by Adrian Schiop, exploring the authenticity through its sociological precision and its choice of non-professional actors. Here, reenactment functions as a documentary gesture of social realism, an attempt to understand the mechanisms of exclusion and power that define an urban periphery.

By contrast, *Ivana the Terrible* shifts the focus inward, and the reenactment tries to document the social environment by investigating personal life. What appears as an ethnographic inquiry into marginal identities in *Soldiers* becomes a psychological and performative exploration of identity itself in *Ivana the Terrible*.

When I first encountered the writings of Ivone Margulies and Sylvie Jasen on reenactment, I recognized aspects of my filmmaking practice. Their reflections helped me understand what I had intuitively explored in *Ivana the Terrible*: how personal trauma can be transformed into shared reflection through the act of performing oneself. Both Margulies and Jasen write about the pedagogical and therapeutic potential of reenactment, how restaging personal or collective wounds can reshape one's relationship with the past. This idea resonated with me. I realized that what Jasen calls reenactment as an event—a process through which the past is not simply reconstructed but continuously reactivated in the present—was in some way what I was doing, even if unconsciously, while making the film.

Margulies's *In Person: Reenactment in Postwar and Contemporary Cinema* (2018) analyzes films in which individuals reenact their own traumas to reclaim agency and reshape memory. I saw a connection to my own experience in her examples: Antonioni's *Attempted Suicide* or Zhang Yuan's *Sons*. Like those protagonists, I was restaging a rupture from my life, using the same people who had been there, in the same spaces where

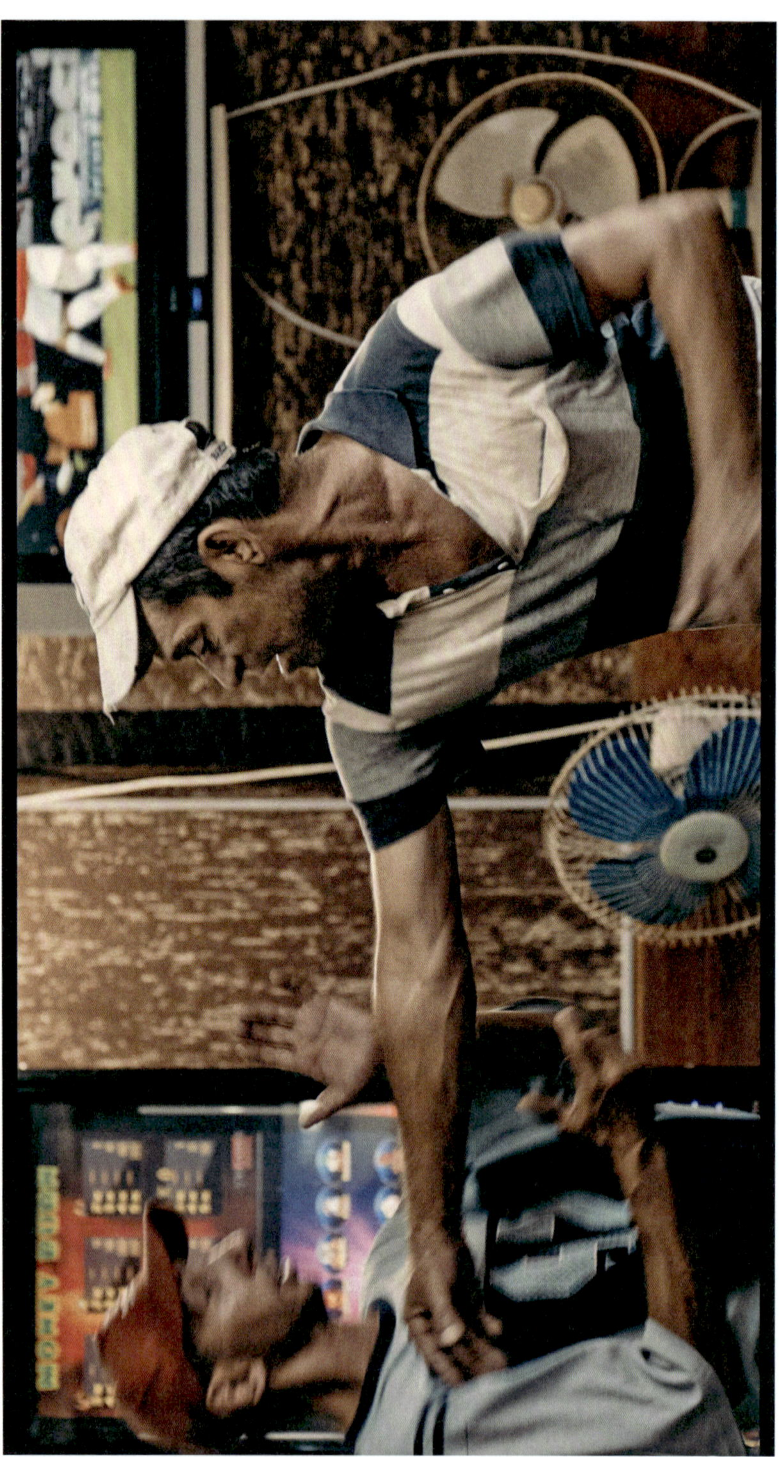

those emotions were lived. In doing so, I was blurring the line between documentary and fiction, authenticity and performance. The result was not a direct representation of what happened, but rather a confrontation between the experience and its reenactment. I began to understand that the authenticity of such work does not depend on factual accuracy but on emotional and moral truth—on the sincerity of repetition.

Jasen's notion of reenactment as an event clarified the experience for me even more. She argues that the meaning of reenactment lies in how the act of repetition reshapes the individual's present. By revisiting my breakdown and the environment that surrounded it, I wasn't simply revisiting the past, I was reinterpreting it. Performing myself turned out to be a way to transform myself in a place, where memory and the present coexist. What began as an exposure of pain became a way to regain control over it. The film thereby performs what Jasen describes as "the transition from private to public," allowing the personal to acquire collective resonance.

This move from self-exposure to shared experience is also what grants the film its pedagogical function. As Margulies notes, reenactment can serve as a "formative process" through which moral or emotional lessons are articulated. In *Ivana the Terrible* humor and irony operate as tools of distance, echoing Brechtian principles of estrangement. This distancing enables both filmmaker and audience to observe the performance of pain without collapsing into it. Rather than seeking catharsis through identification, the film cultivates reflection through ambivalence, the laughter that accompanies discomfort, the self-deprecating tone that transforms vulnerability into agency. Involving my family and friends was crucial. It destabilized the usual hierarchy of authorship and turned the filmmaking process into a collective act of understanding. Their presence made the film alive, unpredictable, and, I think, more honest.

The film's oscillation between sincerity and parody also challenges traditional hierarchies of truth and fiction. As André Bazin warned in his critique of Zavattini's *L'amore in città,* authenticity fetishized for its own sake can "disfigure truth." Yet in *Ivana the Terrible,* I tried to embrace performance as a form of truth-telling, to construct a "truthful fiction"—a cinematic space where exaggeration, humor, and theatricality coexist with genuine emotional exposure. The reenacted scenes

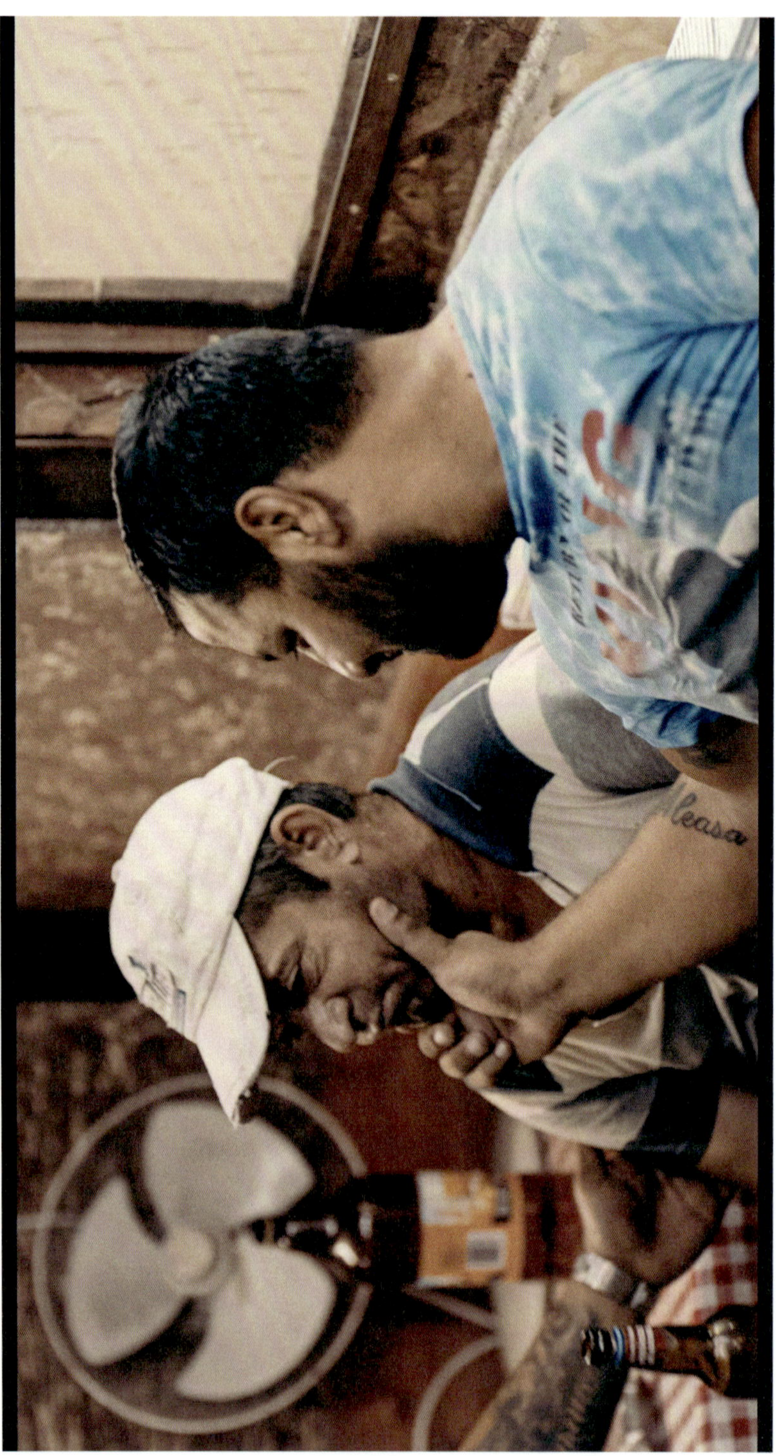

thus operate as a form of psychodrama: therapeutic in intent but also analytic, exposing the mechanisms of both memory and filmmaking. The reenactment, therefore, is not a return to the past but a means of reforming it: a living, performative encounter that reshapes memory through presence.

At Night *Writers' Room* Beatrice Gibson with Denna Cartamkhoob, Xiaolu Guo, Amy Gwatkin, Sophie Robinson

Denna How are you doing?

Bea Good, I enjoyed reading the script so much. I mean, I see a lot of little bits and pieces to fix—even big things to fix, but I think it's really got something.

Denna Yes!

Bea I'm pleased. I hadn't looked at it for ages properly—I had a really focused moment with it.

Denna It's definitely good, reading it through after a while and understanding what could be changed.

Bea I really like the animal bit, I like ... the stuff between Didi and Katia, they feel quite connected. I like their sort of weirdly parallel, supportive relationship, even though they don't—even though it's not literal, if you know what I mean? They're there together.

Denna Yeah, they sort of mirror each other a lot. I liked—there was one thing I sort of noticed about it last time I read it, when Katia leaves and walks out, goes on the walk, it's the same as when Didi ...

Bea Yeah, it's the same walk, through Chinatown.

Denna I thought, visually that could be great.

Bea Totally. There's definitely lots of little things to play with in that sense, like, other repetitions.

Denna Oh yeah, for sure. Okay, so Sophie's running a little bit late and Xiaolu and Amy have just come in.

[The group chat about everyone's location and the weather]

Bea Okay, I guess, well Denna and I had this idea—I'm sure you've all read the script, so you can see how collectively composed it is. And I was quite interested in taking that idea a bit further—I was interested in pushing the idea of a more collectively written or worked on script. Not only collectively written in the sense of people's personal contributions, but also that we might work on it together as a team, as in a kind of writers' room.

Xiaolu Yeah.

Bea The kind of thing that happens more in a TV context, I suppose.

Xiaolu It sounds amazing. I'm not unfamiliar, you know, with this way of working, Bea.

Bea Yes.

Xiaolu It's a wonderful way of working. I mean, of course, I think the people involved have to be totally cool about it, but I think that it's a really authentic way to organize story and characters. The script is already very, very strong.

Bea Thank you.

Xiaolu Yeah, I mean, some parts [are] amazing, the monologues for example. Usually monologue[s] from a writer's point of view are slightly impenetrable and we only accept monologue when we're really far in. But in your case, I think, maybe because there's familiarity, you sort of know who's who, so there's an acceptance immediately, you know?

And I think ... I don't know, I shouldn't take over, you should talk about it first ...

Bea No, I mean, that's sort of ... the thing you were saying about the personal, I'm interested in—in this session in particular—in stepping away from that a bit, in a way, and in looking—because all of us here have certain skills as writers and filmmakers—in looking at the script as a piece of fiction.

Because there's sort of two levels to it, there's this personal material that is a very key part of it, but ultimately, it's also a script, a fiction, and eventually it will be a film. For a viewer, for a spectator, they're not going to know what's real and what's not real. And it's irrelevant, in a way, isn't it? This is why I invited you three specifically to this session and not the other authors or participating characters, because you all have a professional history and this specific skillset. So for me it would be really interesting to look at the script from an entirely fictional point of view, and to kind of feed back on it or to get your responses in that context—if it's possible to divorce those two things, the personal and the fictional—or the formal [laughs]. Especially given that you're all in it as well! You'll notice that Denna and I have also put ourselves in it, too.

Amy In they go.

Xiaolu [laughs] It's really funny, you know, the course I'm teaching at UCL film department is called docufiction, and it's exactly this way of reconstructing real material, making fiction, from the real, you know? And I was like, this should be the course led by you, because ...

Bea [laughs]

Xiaolu It's self-demonstrative, you know, just with the script, you know.

Bea Another interesting thing is, like, that we're constructing this written script, but we're not—I don't think that people will learn these lines and repeat them like you would normally use a script, if you know what I mean? So it's almost like we are making something just to be read. I mean, the process isn't black and white. We'll definitely try to cover everything that's sketched out in a scene, but it's not like I'm going to say, "Okay Amy, can you now learn exactly what you wrote down and repeat it verbatim?" So in this context, it's also, like, what is this object we're making and what for? I don't—like, it sort of exists ...

Xiaolu Of course, yeah.

Bea ... as a writerly object in and of itself.

Denna It still has to be convincing as a feature film, as a script on paper, at least for funding purposes.

Bea Yes, true, of course.

Xiaolu So ... I guess, maybe one thing I thought, it's a very bold script. It starts no-nonsense, straight away, and that's, like, the best in a way. But I guess for a feature film we also need a certain introduction and a sympathy to the characters first.

Bea Yes.

Xiaolu I felt there's a history of the characters that I'm missing, which is crucial for the audience, who has no clue who these people are.

Bea Yes.

Xiaolu So the history of the character ... I think, you know, you're never going to make a conventional film, Bea, you will never make a traditional film. But still, I think I was very disoriented [for] the first 20 pages, I have to say. I didn't understand who Didi was.

I think her being a Black woman, which made her so furious about certain topics, was almost like ... I had to identify the character through my own effort, by linking her history as a Black woman to a more deprived background, you know? And I think I put my sympathy into that absent history, tried to make up her character, her past to compensate.

When Didi talked about her childhood, and then when Katia, for example, talked about when she was giving birth to her daughter Chloe, then about when she was six, seven years old, with her dad or her mum, and I suddenly got a sense of their history—and for me, that came a bit late. I was basically a little lost in the first 25 minutes, you know, I lost that more intensified emotion, but later on [it] became really intense again. Didi's monologue is wonderful, amazing. But like, it's too delayed, you know?

Bea Yeah.

Xiaolu But then this is the first draft, of course. I think you might want to have some organic scenes, you know, a monologue or something that refers to people's pasts more, you know? Didi, a scene of Didi talking about a memory of when she was 10 or something, or, and Katia ...

Bea Yes, I was thinking about, actually, Denna, do you—I'm having a mind blank—do you remember the film Tim told us to watch with the multiple characters set in LA, the big Hollywood feature?

Denna Yes, oh my god, hang on ...

Bea The one where the plane flies over the city in the beginning and it's that that connects all the characters ...

Amy Altman?

Bea and Denna Yes.

Amy What's it called?

Denna Yes.

Bea It has this very amazing introduction of all the characters at the beginning, interweaving with each other via the planes.

Amy *Shorts*, something *Shorts* ...

Denna Yeah, yeah, *Short Cuts*.

Amy *Short Cuts*.

Bea Yes!

Xiaolu It's great, it's great. But it's also very busy, a very fast film.

Bea But you get what I'm saying, why I'm relating it to what you're saying, Xiaolu, because you get—in a very short space of time—you get a small sense of who each character is.

Amy Weirdly, conversely, I quite enjoyed not being told someone's background and having it emerge. And I felt like one thing that I got from the whole thing, very visually, was this idea of, like, a fluidity linking things—it is a little bit abstract, you know, so I guess I was imagining it a bit like how a camera might move through scenes, like how we might move from person to person.

Bea Exactly.

Amy I actually really liked being dropped in the middle of, you know, what could be quite a harrowing abortion scene and then there being these elements, I felt like we were encouraged to sort of tease out a story or a background ourselves and I didn't mind that I wasn't told. And I also thought Didi comes ... I think she comes across really well.

Xiaolu Yeah.

Amy One of the questions was about the necessity of "a protagonist," and I think she's—well, she's quite straight-talking if you think how theatrical some of the other characters are.

Xiaolu Sorry, so just to help me to know a bit more, so Didi's character is based on which person? I guess it was just very abstract for me to begin with, also because of my background, you know, it's like you reading a Chinese script. For someone non-British it took me a while to enter. I'm an experimental person, but still I need to just identify what's what! [laughs]

Bea Yes, of course.

Denna But I felt that too. We've talked about that, haven't we, Bea?

Bea Yes, we totally have.

Denna Having a bit more backstory to the characters, to Didi and Katia in particular.

Xiaolu I think it would make the script much stronger. When you're shooting, you might even completely abandon it, the background, because the actor would know where they come from.

Bea Yes.

Xiaolu But now, for [the] moment, in this context, if the audience is having to guess, you lose them, you know? I mean, I can look in amazement at a work of art for 10 minutes in a gallery, but after that I need to sit down. So, for example, [the] Xiaolu Guo character, my character, you know, the first time she appears, it's in the bookshop, right? Talking about love.

Bea Yes.

Xiaolu Of her—it's a passage from my book, and that's fine. But then I thought, "That's the introduction of her position, her identity as a novelist and as a Chinese person."

The next thing is a conversation about being in the world as a woman, you know, the loss of sexual passion is a theme, the idea that it becomes more about another thing, about wellbeing and ... it's about the embodiment of love in real life, not fantasy, in childcare, caring for a child etc. But then I thought, "Who is this person?"—in a way, you should rescue her, me, [laughs], Xiaolu Guo, as a character, instead of her long speeches, you know?

[Sophie joins the Zoom]

Xiaolu Hi Sophie, hi, sorry, I'm just going to finish my thought quickly. Just, you know, if you want to rescue my character—because at the moment Xiaolu just could just be cut, we don't care about her, this Chinese woman.

You don't want to cut her when we know more about her, say, Xiaolu Guo, this Chinese writer who came from a total[ly] abusive childhood—I was adopted and then I was given back, and then my father was in a Cultural Revolution labor camp forever, and then I grew up with my totally violent mother beating me up all the time, and then I ran away at 18 because China was opening up.

So there's sexual abuse, a totally violent and loveless childhood, a running away from China, from the censorship, to London. And being here, trying to establish myself as an artist, making my way as an artist, but refusing to be a low-class immigrant. Not letting the immigrant identity define me.

Bea I see, yes.

Xiaolu I want to be defined as artist rather than immigrant. And I think that, that I would, that Xiaolu Guo character would have more depth this way.

Bea Yeah, definitely.

Xiaolu She would be rescued, you know what I mean? This is what I'm trying to say. So I think the same would need to happen with Therese and all the other characters, if you want to keep these characters, if you want to keep Therese character.

Bea Therese is very light at the moment, isn't she?

Xiaolu You need to write her, because what I know about Therese is beyond simply a blonde, beautiful Danish girl.

Bea Yeah, of course.

Xiaolu Her life has been confused by love. In a way it's bleak, as a beautiful, blonde, young Danish girl, you know? And I think that's something that is missing for her. That's why I think the Katia character in the middle of the story saying, "Who gives a damn about Virginia Woolf?" Nothing is taken for granted, you know? Her violent attitude against a white, British novelist, we need to feel that. You know, coming from the deep depression each woman is in, is going through, right? Whether you're white or Black, right? So that's all I want to say, we need the history of the characters, you know, blonde, Danish, Chinese, Black, white, artist, this is what we need.

Bea It's challenging thinking about how to do that because everyone's so interesting, I mean, in my mind they could all have their own feature film [laughs], you know? If you really go down that road, what are the limits?

Xiaolu But I think it's amazing, and you have space, Bea, because you have a lot of space to make each character grounded a bit more. And then after that, you go somewhere more abstract.

Bea Yeah, yeah, yeah, I think you're right.

I'm just going to recap really quickly what I said for Sophie, which was along the lines of this Zoom being a way to bring everyone who's already sort of semi-involved with the film and who comes from a particular writerly or filmmaking background, to bring all those people together to look at the script as more of a fictional object, to sort of try and helicopter a bit over the personal—or the way that it's personally constructed, and to critique it as a sort of fictional object. So we'll see how this Zoom goes and everyone's different input, but it also would be really interesting for me to sort of mirror the way the film's constructed and the way it's also written.

I'm really interested in the idea of a writers' room, this TV format, and in how much more I might be able to push this collective writing thing. Because that's way more exciting to me than a Beatrice Gibson script, which this already isn't.

So that's a little structural intro, basically. So it would be really helpful if we could start just going through everyone's general response to the script. It's a first draft, so it's got some legs, I think, but there's definitely some work to do, too. [laughs]

Sophie Sorry I was late, I'm really happy to be here. Honestly, I love the script, I'm really excited.

Bea Oh good. I'm so happy to hear that. I'm excited also by Xiaolu's immediate reference to herself as "Xiaolu character," that's going to be my new—that's gonna be the way I refer to everybody, like, "Bea character," "Sophie character." [laughs]

Xiaolu Totally, totally.

Denna Denna character. [laughs]

Amy The minute she said that, I was like, "Oh my god, that's so helpful."

Bea Isn't it? It just completely encapsulates the ... that's exactly what it is!

Xiaolu I think, you know, that's the way I wrote all these books. I really know, you know, you're in the book, everyone is, you know, my life, my child, myself, there's the child character, that's the husband character, or whatever, mother character. They all hate me in the end for putting them in there, so it doesn't really matter.

The momentum of the script is really strong, Bea. I think there is something very no bullshit, you know, and that is quite amazing. I think not one scene is a fake, wasted, or just a wishy-washy scene. So Bea, Denna, I think that's really the core of your script, it's beautiful.

Bea Thank you.

Xiaolu And it's totally sincere, you know? The attitude is completely ... I mean, the only thing is for me, as I mentioned, is the history of the characters, flesh them out more, really just go there, explore them more.

Bea So you mean ... Would you say that in relation to the entire structure—sorry, not just at the beginning, you mean, really pull out these characters throughout? Or was it a comment in relation to ...

Xiaolu The beginning and the middle are slightly abstract, but then from the middle onward it's very strong, the monologue—somehow, I suddenly was in.

Bea Which monologue are you talking about in particular?

Amy The big one, the three-page one?

Xiaolu Oh yeah, that's amazing. [laughs]

Bea There's quite a lot of monologues. [laughs]

Xiaolu I love it, I love it.

Denna Didi's first monologue?

Xiaolu Yeah.

Denna Yeah, that's her talking to Lily, isn't it, in the house?

Xiaolu Yeah.

Denna Incredible, yeah.

Xiaolu I feel like in this script you have, I don't know how many, maybe eight women or something or whatever, they're all in a way speaking about women's experience, you know? And it could be just one face, or 10 face[s], talking about how we're united in this womanhood, you know? I just ... yes, mention this, I just wonder maybe in the future you could do something very radical in a way, you know, based on those raw materials.

Amy Did Didi write the monologue? I just wondered—everyone kind of—each character sort of wrote their own script?

Bea Yes, totally, I mean, they're in some ways verbatim, but then they're also quite heavily edited by me afterward just to make everything flow, or to be a bit more precise. I take out quite a lot.

Denna Amy, do you want to respond a bit, share your overall thoughts? And we can sort of go round and discuss them together, is that good, Bea?

Bea Yes, let's do that.

Amy I guess I was thinking it through with the questions that you'd sort of posed, which I found really helpful as a way of kind of logging my thoughts. Like I said, I really like the connections between, how one thing leads to another, and the *Short Cuts* reference is good, actually. And I also thought, the way that you immediately start with dream imagery, that's pretty helpful, too I think, because then not only do you kind of create a bit of an ambiguity around things—which maybe you want to—but also means you have a bit of latitude with things not making sense.

Bea Yeah, exactly, yeah.

Amy And I focused—I really tried to work out what the connection between Didi and Katia was. And I thought, "Okay, so Katia first appears in a dream, which then turns out to be reality. Did Didi somehow manifest her?" And then at some point I was like, "Is Didi, like, her mother?" It's a bit like a mother-daughter reincarnation of ...

Bea Well, they have that really mad conversation at the end, don't they, where Katia's talking about being a single child.

Amy That's the one!

Bea And then Didi—sort of—yeah.

Amy That's when I was like, "Aha, it's her own mum."

And then, I guess, like I said, I thought Didi's voice is really refreshingly straightforward. A lot of the other character[s] that kind of appear, say stuff which is very theatrical or ... it just feels a bit more jazzy, and then she's got quite a believable, or like, emotional role. I felt most emotionally attached to Didi. But I suppose she's also there most, isn't she? And then, I suppose, I was wondering what or who are all the other characters? Like ... are they all like, lessons in, or are they all different facets of how you could navigate ...?

Bea I can tell you—the trajectory was very much not wanting to have any protagonists, it was about wanting just to have a crowd.

Amy Right.

Bea But then realizing that, like, you know, for something of that duration, feature-length, you do sort of need "a girl and a gun," as Godard used to say, you need something—even if it's a ruse, to draw people in. You do need something—choral is pretty hard to pull off in feature form. So then Katia and Didi emerged as, like, a viable pair of protagonists. But I definitely want to keep the chorality. Many women. This was always the key idea.

Xiaolu Yes, I really support your collective portrait, and that's the only way to get away from conventional, one woman's sad reality, you know, some kind of narration of motherhood and pain. That is, again, another victim through a single narration, you know? So I like your collective portrait, but I think ... so then—it means you really need to develop more, beyond Didi and Katia. I think Katia's [story] also needs to be a bit developed, you know, quite developed.

Bea Yeah.

Xiaolu We might need more of her background history. You have space, enough space to write about their ... almost like ... don't worry about convention, the key is to understand where people are from.

Yeah, so you might have some tough work to sort of pull the strings of all the women together a little earlier. I mean, not as a traditional introduction, but as kind of impressionistic introduction, you know, structure-wise.

Bea Hmm, substantial enough introductions.

Xiaolu So we see a bit more of a masterful structuring of all these people that might later appear in the film.

Bea For example, I thought the bookstore scene, when I was reading it this morning, I thought, "Why are we meeting Xiaolu so late?" Actually, we should meet—like *Short Cuts*—you sort of should meet everybody initially somehow before. Because when you suddenly come across new characters, you're like, who is this?

Actually, Sophie, on another note, totally, I realized I had totally failed you or your character when I read it this morning, because I was like, "Oh my god, Sophie doesn't drink," and we're like meeting her opening a bottle of wine in her apartment.

Sophie [Laughs] I didn't mind at all, I was really into my scenes. But I guess I wanted to add to what's being talked about, and to say that, like, I think I—basically—I thought the monologues were brilliant, I love the characters of Didi and Katia, I really ... and I think it's really important and powerful that you included one of the most difficult parts of our previous workshop.

Bea Yeah.

Sophie Thought it was great, the way it's been done. And I ... and, like, the way that it isn't really resolved, you know, the way it just kind of hangs? It's important because ... I think that, I suppose I was thinking about conversations, and I was thinking that even though I adored some of the monologues—and I do think that as well there is a possibility to do those, like, dreamier scenes, or to have something happen—to sometimes have the monologue be straight to camera and sometimes have the monologue be ... to have the visuals also doing some exposition or doing some, like, dreamwork, or adding some vibes to the whole thing at the same time.

Bea Yes.

Sophie But I also basically love the conversations and the ways in which details about characters get drawn out in dialogue. I think that's really cool. Because I also think it's like ... I don't know, I was thinking about the Bechdel Test and the way that, like, so many films fail to demonstrate two women talking to each other about anything other than men, you know?

Bea [laughs]

Sophie So I think it's really nice—and I also think we're quite a self-obsessed culture, and I really love the writer Rachel Cusk and the way that in Rachel Cusk's novels all of the stories are drawn out through this anonymous narrator's conversations with people. I just think it's a radical act to have a conversation with somebody, especially when you don't agree, or, you know, you're coming from different places. I even thought that there could be more of that. I think that's also a way of drawing out, that would also be another way to draw out ...

Bea Personal details, yeah.

Sophie Yeah, without just being like, "I was born in x and this happened," because I think it would just be a dynamic way of maybe fleshing out some of the characters if that's ... fleshing out some of the choral characters.

Amy Yeah, I like that idea.

Denna I wanted to ...

Bea Can I just say one thing? Sorry Denna, I wanted to say one thing about the ... it's also peppered with these much more documentary moments with characters I haven't met yet, who are people who work in the or at night. And those—I wanted to just flag that those scenes are really light and need a lot of development because they haven't been cast yet—they will all be street cast, and so I don't know who those people are yet. So for me those are really quite clunky at the moment.

For example, the scene where the person in the subway is making a list, I think in a way that's the most successful of those extra characters because it is so abstract, like, this weird almost robotic poetic thing, but the others try to be something a bit more intimate and fail. Like, yeah, the one with the sex worker, for example, is really annoying, isn't it? Because it's totally fabricated.

Amy I thought that was a bit plonked in there, that was all I was going to say about that.

Bea Exactly.

Amy That's what you're saying. But the list on the subway, is that the cleaner?

Bea Yeah, who talks about the pattern of their day.

Amy Yeah.

Denna And that's nice, the way Katia's list mirrors that moment as well ... What I was just going to say about the lack of conversation is something we did sort of ... we were looking at, weren't we? Because there were so many monologues. And that conversation at the end between Didi and Katia was a sort of a response to sending them both a series of questions and then constructing a possible conversation with their answers. So maybe—and I think that it works, actually, it's working really well—so maybe it's more of that that we need to do between characters.

Xiaolu I think so, yes. For example, I think Xiaolu character and Denna character, I think we could, you know, maybe have a conversation about sex as an overrated concept. Or, women's sexual appeal, women's sexual experience, like, you know, this could be debated through my character and some other character. And also, I quite like Denna character's position when she says, "Oh, I'm just not in a stage of thinking about that kind of love or romantic engagement." And I think really, you know, it's very interesting, woman as kind of ground ... almost like, you know, the idea of nature, the mother, the woman always there, grounding, not only jumping around, chasing erotic love or sexual passion.

Bea Yes, I really like the multiplicity of positions you get in that scene.

Xiaolu Yeah.

Bea Because you never—I like the contrast, basically, of people who are very sexually active and others who are—because you don't really, no one ever really admits that they're not having that much sex [laughs], do they? So I'll do that then, I'll step in and admit that for everyone. [laughs]

Xiaolu I think that now we really can. I mean, Bea character could also be having the conversation about that, right?

Bea Yeah.

Xiaolu And also, I remember when I was reading Katia's experience of being ... What's the word? Of her emergency cesarean, you know, that was exactly my experience, too. Of course, Katia character knew nothing about my experience, so she, you, the audience might think, you know, ah that woman with an easygoing ... you know, flying around, with her bohemian life. But, it could be ... it could create a sort of opaque judgemental emotion from the audience, you know? In a way, you can say, "Okay, I don't care about audience," but on the other hand, we do want to reach the audience, the ones who don't understand us, right? So I think my character just—[laughs] actually, I come from the same position, I had a cesarean, an awful one, I couldn't get over it, actually, fuck—can't we look at things intellectually, do we have to go through psychoanalysis each time, so that we're forever being pinned down, infantalized as human beings, you know, go through childhood, experience trauma again, again, again, and then again, again, you know? It could be—I'm just saying, it could be also debunked, you know, that kind of view. And then, say, my character can bring out [laughs] my horror of a cesarean, the death of parents, and worse, the abortion experience in China, which is opposite, treating birth in a completely different way, you know?

Bea I remember being so struck by that, I remember meeting you in London Fields and we were talking about it and you were like, "Abortion in China" during the One Child Policy era was like an everyday casual event.'

Xiaolu Yeah, and that is just completely unthinkable for the liberal Western society in a way, you know? So I think it might make things broader, more international, in a positive sense, you know?

Bea I mean, there is ... at the end scene between Katia and Didi, where they're discussing, Katia's saying, "Well, actually, for me having a Black family is radical," whereas Didi's taken this opposite position and doesn't want to ...

Xiaolu That's good.

Bea I'm really taken by those divergent positions, having them co-exist.

Xiaolu That's really good, yes.

Sophie Yeah, I definitely think there's things to be brought out in conversation. I was also thinking about some of the stuff that Adam said in the previous workshop about ... I think it was in relation to marriage and parenting and old age, right? And that's, it's like, a legitimate worry. Thinking about non-traditional family structures or non-biological family, and how that relates to queerness and queer communities of care. But it also kind of ties into some of the conversations we were having around childcare. But, yeah, I was thinking that fundamentally conversation could be a way to draw some of those perspectives out. And again, there's a flipside, or underside to freedom, and that's loneliness or lack of care ... or something.

Sorry, it feels like I'm not making that much sense, but I think that was one of the conversations I remember having with you all that struck me.

Bea Definitely.

Sophie Toward the end of the last session, which I thought was really interesting, I was like "Who's going to take care of me?", basically.

Denna Yeah.

Bea Yeah, because Adam had, or was talking about, a specific physical condition in relation to that as well.

Denna I suppose one thing that other people have mentioned when they've read the script is that there's a lot of talking, there's a lot of monologues. So a lot can come out in conversation, but also ...

Bea Where are these conversations happening? In what context?

Denna Yeah, and, like, is it ... ? We sort of also need more visual stuff and more quiet stuff to balance it all out, because in the end, it's a film, not a book.

Bea And also, it's got this, like, in a way, very generative but also quite restrictive frame, like, it's one night, and there's only so many places we can go—I'm like, "Where else is open? Where would be open at 4am?" [laughs] Trying to imagine ... or, I guess the flashbacks are doing that work also—the dreamy parts are helping get into other spaces while staying within that quite singular restricted frame.

Sophie Maybe some of the—I guess, maybe some of that could be, like, moving ... to move away from something that's too dialogue-heavy, some of the things that are coming up could be shown through ... I guess there's a focus on types of labor throughout, right?

Bea Yes.

Sophie And a lot—even from the beginning, like, the comparison of the butcher and the abortion. And some of the characters in it that haven't been cast yet, like, there's a lot of focus on various kinds of domestic and non-domestic labor. And some of the exposition and also a way of getting—away—revealing more about character and history without too much effort, without being too dialogue-heavy could be shots of somebody doing their job, basically. Shots of people wiping down bars, or some of the "night-worker[s] on the metro story" could be told through a series of shots of them just doing their job, you know?

Bea Yeah, yeah, that would be beautiful.

Sophie Something that feels quite kinetic or repetitive, I think the same thing with childcare and, like, the bath, and the ways—I suppose, thinking about imminent labor, like, imminent labor and this idea of repetition.

Bea That's beautiful, I really love that.

Sophie I was wondering also about the Alice Notley character, Beatrice.

Bea Alice!

Sophie Is she—is that text from ... I meant to look it up but I didn't have time.

Bea It's from *The Descent of Alette*, yes. The film is really influenced by that poem, so I wanted to get it in there. The trajectory for everyone, the internal journeys at the center of the script, the journey through the night and the eternal journey in the psyche—the stuff that everybody is dealing with, going deeper and deeper into and down into the world of dreams, away from the intellectual or the rational. That's pure Alice.

Sophie Is that her only scene?

Bea Yeah, but only because it's a bit difficult for her to do anything else these days, with her knee.

Sophie Yeah.

Bea She just wants to read poems. I love her. Every time I say, "Would you like to come and do a development Zoom or a meeting in relation to your character", she's like, "Nope, I just want to read my poems. If you want to film me reading poems, I'll do that." [laughs]

Sophie [laughs]

Xiaolu That brings me [to] a question, which is very, in a way, crucial for me to help your script.

Bea Yeah.

Xiaolu Which is a very practical question, what—I know it's very early stage, what do you—how do you think ... will you mix the real characters with actors?

Bea Hmm.

Xiaolu Or will you get all the real [people] as [often] as you can to play themselves? Because that approach will change your script.

Bea Yes, I know. I keep trying to work with actors and I just can't seem to do it. [Laughts] I'm not anti it, I just ... every time I do stuff with them, it just doesn't feel anything like as good as when I'm able to do—working—talking to real people. I don't know, we tried, didn't we, Denna? We tried for the protagonist to be a total construction, we tried—we had a series of castings and it just ...

Xiaolu Yeah.

Bea It just felt so wooden compared to ...

Xiaolu ... the real thing.

Bea To the real thing, yeah. So, I don't know.

Xiaolu Yeah, I mean, I ask the question just because from my experience, you know, making all these films, writing all these novels, I face exactly the same issue. Let's just say, you know, write a novel, you know, I never want to write a novel because I don't believe the conventional narrative, so I write it with real names. But then they'll sue me, of course, in the end.

What I tend to do is I decide, "Okay, this is a memoir piece," then I tell my publisher a certain name is changed, but most of the name[s] remain real, or I just can't get through it. Then, at the end, I have to change all the names. And when I change all their names, I tell my publisher, "Actually it's not memoir, it's a novel." I gain this huge freedom as fiction, because I think the form doesn't trap me. And I remember one book, you know, one of my earlier books, when I decided, "I just can't get by, they're going to have trouble with me," then I just changed all the names into fiction. Then I started to re-write every character, and actually, in a way it improves immensely because you then have this freedom [to] make up the stuff that you can't write in a real form. But, you know, or the other way round for you, you can only work with the real person, then that's really the solid weight for you, in a way, for your film.

And I thought about all of this when I read your script, I thought this could change [the film] a lot, you know?

Bea But the interesting thing is, you know, I was saying to Katia, "How are you feeling?" She said it, she was like, "No one's going to know that it's me". So in a way it is fiction, because only we know that it's based on real characters. I mean, nobody knows, the audience doesn't know who we are. I mean, maybe it depends slightly on whether you have a public dimension to your life, but, you know, most of us are purely anonymous. And in a way, it is highly, highly crafted, like, I have put you all in certain locations and made certain things happen, and constructed certain situations and certain conversations.

Amy Yeah, it goes back to what Xiaolu said about the Xiaolu character, really. Take Amy character. As soon as you look at it like that, you realize how ... Because I suppose, from my point of view, it's this particular facet, like, it's—weirdly, all the stories I told were about this one particular affair that was not of huge importance to me in reality.

Bea [laughs]

Amy But, I mean, it's just like, one view of something. And I like that you put me in a bar, I think that was great—or put Amy character in a bar.

Bea Have you seen *Variety* by Bette Gordon? [laughs]

Amy I have, yeah. [laughs]

Bea I just want to be in that bar all the time with all those women [laughs], so I thought I'd put you all in one.

Amy I've worked in bars a lot and I love working in bars, so that's really my ... I feel very comfortable behind the bar. And I think it's quite ... I don't know, I think there's quite a nice counterpoint, because lots of characters are saying lots of, like, much deeper and more vulnerable-making things, like, it's maybe good that there's a balance or tension between this quite kind of trivial, boozy, or fake, or surface feeling and the rest.

The way I actually remembered telling that story in the video was quite a sort of jokey flattening way of saying something, something which is dark or painful or traumatic, and that seems appropriate. I like that.

And I like that maybe that's quite realistic —that that exists if you're having a conversation about things which are dark and traumatic, it's not always real for everyone to talk about difficulties with real candor and real self-awareness ... I don't know.

Bea Very true, yeah, I love to crack a joke when I'm relaying trauma.

The script for *At Night* was developed collectively over the course of 2021 to 2026. It features contributions from Diocouda Diaoune, Alice Notley, Katia Belo Cardosa, Sophie Robinson, Amy Gwatkin, Lily McMenamy, Adam Christensen, Denna Cartamkhoob, Pauline Curnier Jardin, Laida Lertxundi, and Beatrice Gibson.

Filmmaking Under the Influence
Rosa Aiello

01

What dominates in my memory are moments that were impossible to capture. My collaborator puts her hand on my lower back as we cross the road, guiding me through a place that is so familiar to me and so foreign to her. I picture how great it would be if we could film that: the repetition of the gesture in different settings, the surprise that must register in my body each time. Believe me when I say that they were the tenderest moments, the tone of which I could never quite figure out (Were they maternal? Were they controlling? Were they snatches of something more intimate?). I was four months pregnant, and more vulnerable than I wanted to admit; and from the moment she found out, I could feel her desire to protect me, though she was half my age.

I could never turn the camera on this gesture, because it was too spontaneous, too fleeting. I had no idea when it would occur, though it happened almost every day. I didn't want to speculate on what it meant to her, to ask viewers to speculate with me, nor to draw her attention to her likely unconscious gesture, to ask her to account for it, as we and the act became conscious, and shy, or at least, then, performing. Not to mention that it was physically impossible to turn the camera on my own back, to frame myself from behind.

I never captured the unfathomable comparisons she made: between my father's hometown in Lamezia Terme and her father's in Inner Mongolia. I never captured the way she affirmed me, my decisions, my partner's driving—the way she told us, although she was meant to be the student and I the teacher, that we were doing well. Neither could I quite fathom this leap she had made, to come to Southern Italy, live for

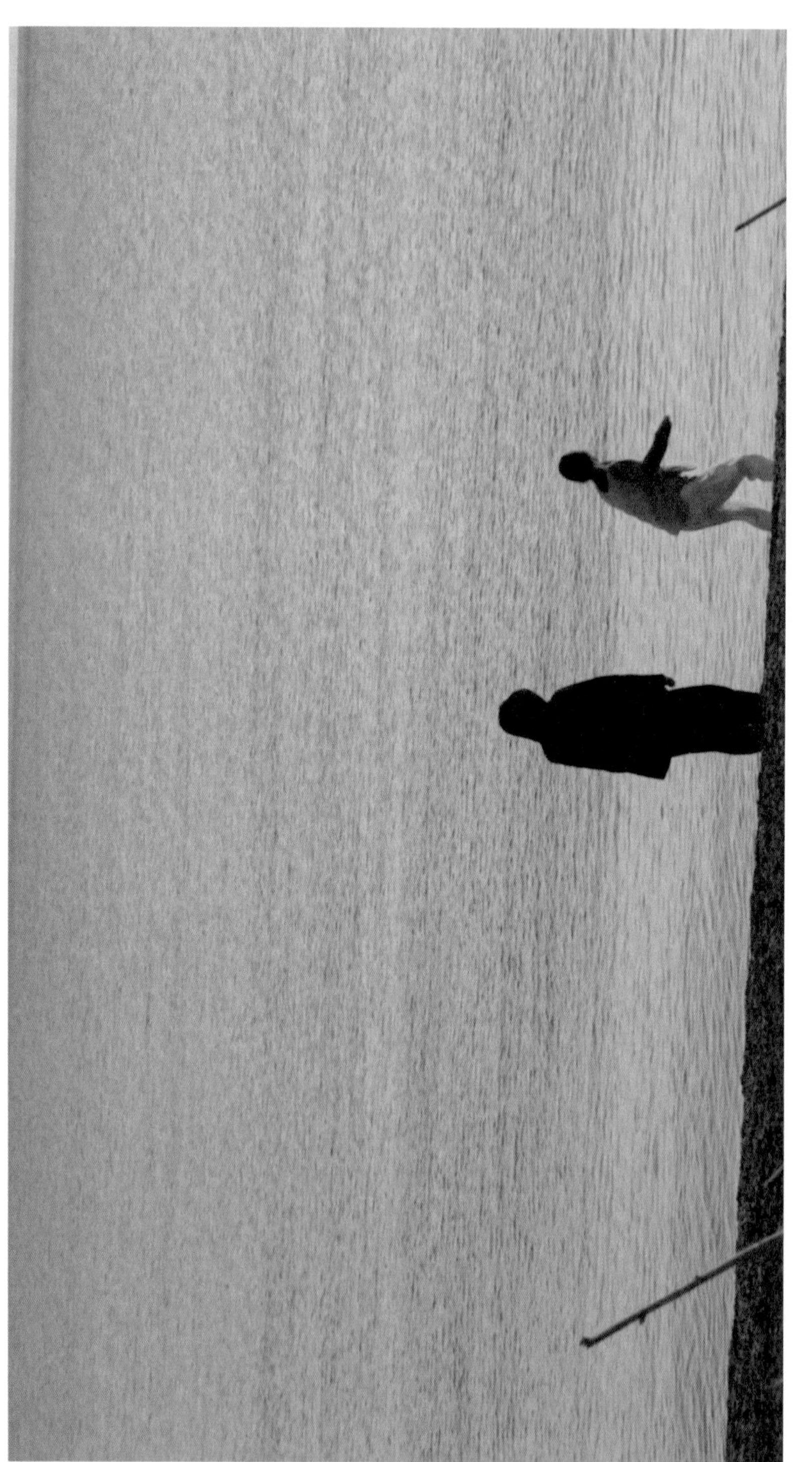

a time in a house with my partner and I, and make a film together. She had contacted me eleven months earlier, asking to work with me as part of her last year of studies for her art degree in London. The email felt like a bolt of lightning—an appearance of something unexpected that shifted my reality, subtly but definitely. I don't mean that anything dramatic occurred during our time working together, and yet, everything changed, the way bodies in space move and orient with an awareness of the nearby presence of other bodies, other consciousnesses.

02

My collaborator arrived at night. It was a stormy April in Lamezia Terme, and the evenings were cold, the palms a frantic wrapping blur in strong winds. I waved at her from where I stood, outside our parked car. She had wanted to take public transportation from the airport, or a taxi, but I explained to her that that was not possible here. The wind beat at her small body as she crossed the distance between us, she was dressed simply and practically in a black rain coat, black backpack, running shoes, her camera strapped across her front.

My collaborator was arriving into an established routine of daily life. I was her host, and it was my pleasure to serve her. We ate pasta with zucchini and fava beans for dinner. We showed her the fat bean pods we had picked that day, expecting her to react with awe. I did not yet know that she preferred sweet things and disliked most vegetables. She ate everything I gave her, dutifully. I showed her my growing belly. She told us of her journey. We made tea and arranged ourselves around the television, as we did every night; and beside our two-person couch, we pulled up an arm chair for her to sit in and a foot rest for her feet. We watched the film *Vertigo*, her choice, and waited for the padding cats to decide anew with whom to settle.

She had come because I had suggested that we investigate a most obvious meeting point of our cultural experiences—the Chinese population of Lamezia Terme, Calabria—and she had agreed. I tried to manage my expectations by saying that the purpose of this period of working, of every period of working, is to whittle a new tool or enlarge a capacity. Indeed, my entire view of Lamezia Terme would change through my collaborator's relations to the city; and my growing ability to retreat in the process would become the fruiting of the method.

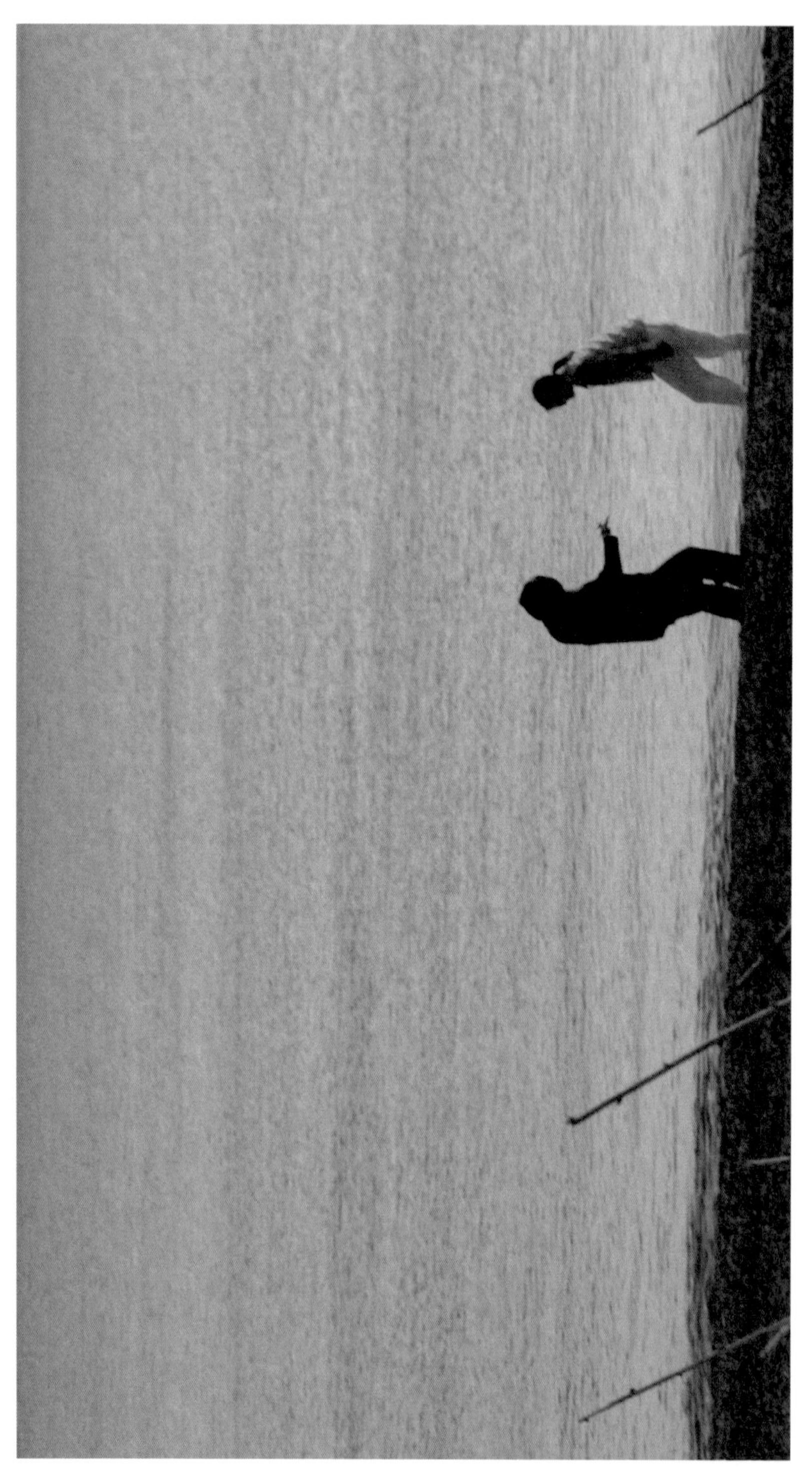

03

I believe people seek each other out, often unconsciously, to serve each other's needs for change. This is both a function of relativity (How do I appear to myself relative to who this other is?), and of what actions and attitudes are demanded by the presence of another. This could be as simple as the need to ask permission, the need to say "good morning," the need to stick to a "yes" in the face of someone's doubt. Being in relation is both inconvenient and incomparably rich.

There was something about the roles I was to occupy in relation to my collaborator that seemed correctly timed. There were many parts of myself I wanted to unlearn before my child was born: I wanted to feel really at home, really competent, really purposeful—as if the birth would set my life wherever I had arrived by then. And so I felt myself scrambling toward wisdom and excellence. I would be the translator, I would be the guide. I would have more perspective, more certainty about my ways of working, needing to put them into words, stand up for them, allow my collaborator in. But because I was pregnant, I was tired, and unreliable, and unpredictable—nothing of what I wanted to be or become. I would have to allow myself to be influenced, not only by my collaborator, but by the conditions, by our errors, our inabilities; which was to take to the extreme an inchoate approach I have had to filmmaking for some years, which I have come to think of as being *in reality.*

The concept "Acknowledge the Cow" comes from an anecdote that Lesley Ewen tells in her course *Developing Performance* at the Royal Academy of Dramatic Art, and that arrived to me via my brother and frequent collaborator, Dylan Aiello. She describes the time she was performing on an open field near a farm. A pregnant cow ambled into the space of the stage, and gave birth, right there, during her performance. Rather than plowing through her lines and actions as written, unchanged by the real events taking place, she righted herself by folding the presence of the cow's giving birth into her performance. Had she ignored it, she would have spent excesses of energy to overcome the moment of destabilization, to compete with the cow for the audience's attention. Instead, she and the piece were literally given life by the unforeseen.

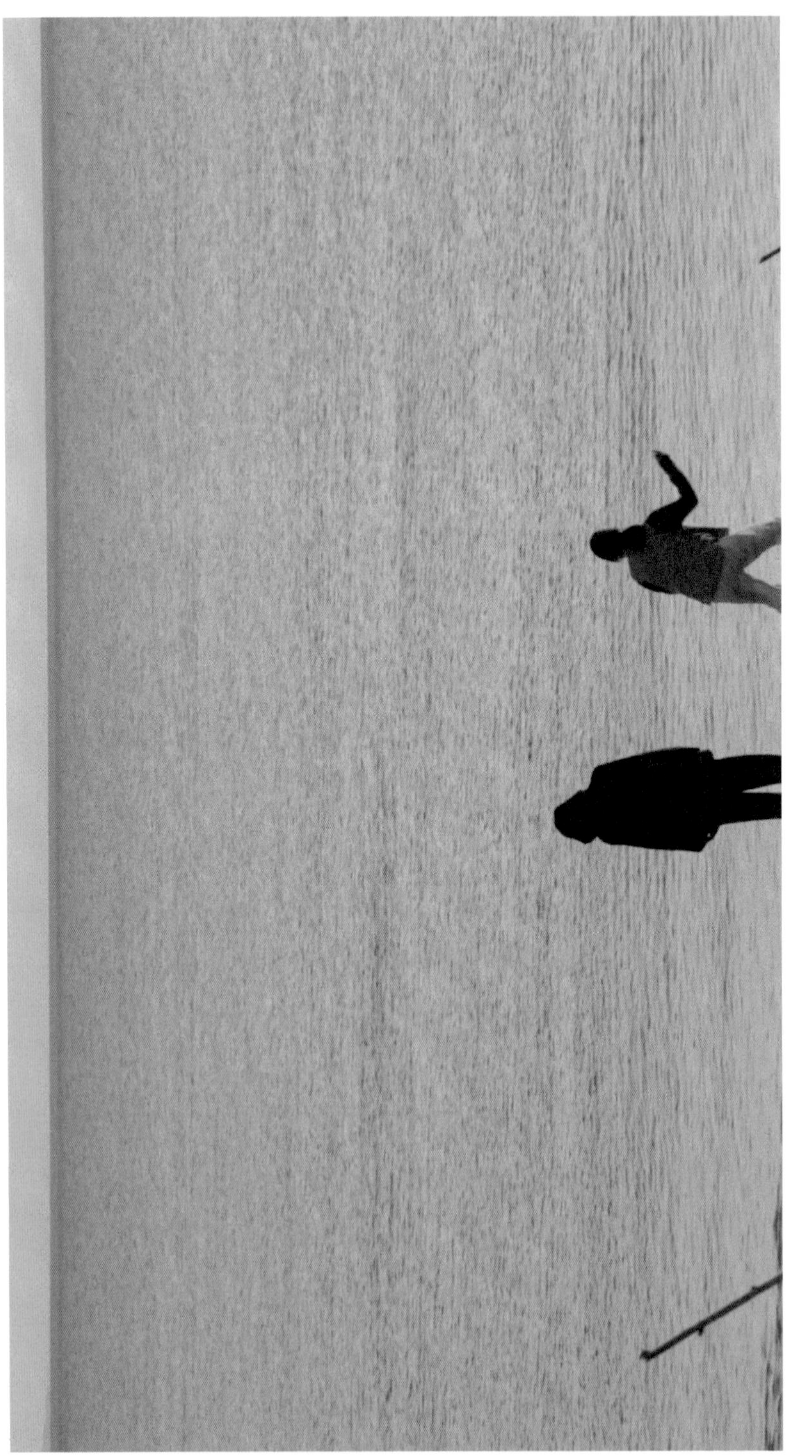

I don't know exactly what Lesley did when she became aware of the cow, or *how* exactly she integrated the interruption, but the spirit of this story has brought me to three points that are the foundation of a method for me:

1. To point out the unexpected, lean into it, repeat it, or highlight it, rather than try to erase or ignore it. Same goes for technical errors and limitations. Same goes for tics of editing, camera, or writing. These may become style.

2. To fold in real life conditions, especially physical states and relationships, e.g. me being pregnant. This doesn't mean to make the work about pregnancy. But to be open to the forms and states that pregnancy introduces.

3. To be ready to see and believe new information, and to change the focus or meaning of the project as this new information demands. Be ready to discard central elements of the original idea.

Just because this total acceptance of reality is the very expertise I wanted to hold up and value for myself and my collaborator, does not mean it felt good, or easy—my actual conditions were unglamorous, and without apparent vision or mastery. We could only work a few hours each day. I needed to stop often, go home early, cut things off before we got in very deep. I needed long periods, sometimes whole days, to recover after strain. Thoughts seemed to slip through my unruly brain, which was, I learned, partially offline as it rearranged itself for motherhood, whole swathes of grey matter shrinking and densifying. I was short-tempered. I lacked drive. I lacked the impulse to persuade. These are the states that pregnancy introduced, and they felt altogether out of sync with the task we had before us.

04

There are stretches of road in Lamezia Terme that seem to bear as a fractal representation, the fact of Calabria's being a peninsula. Surface areas for semi-regulated arrival, construction, and commerce, and a fragmented identity that for centuries has had to do with an ever-forged

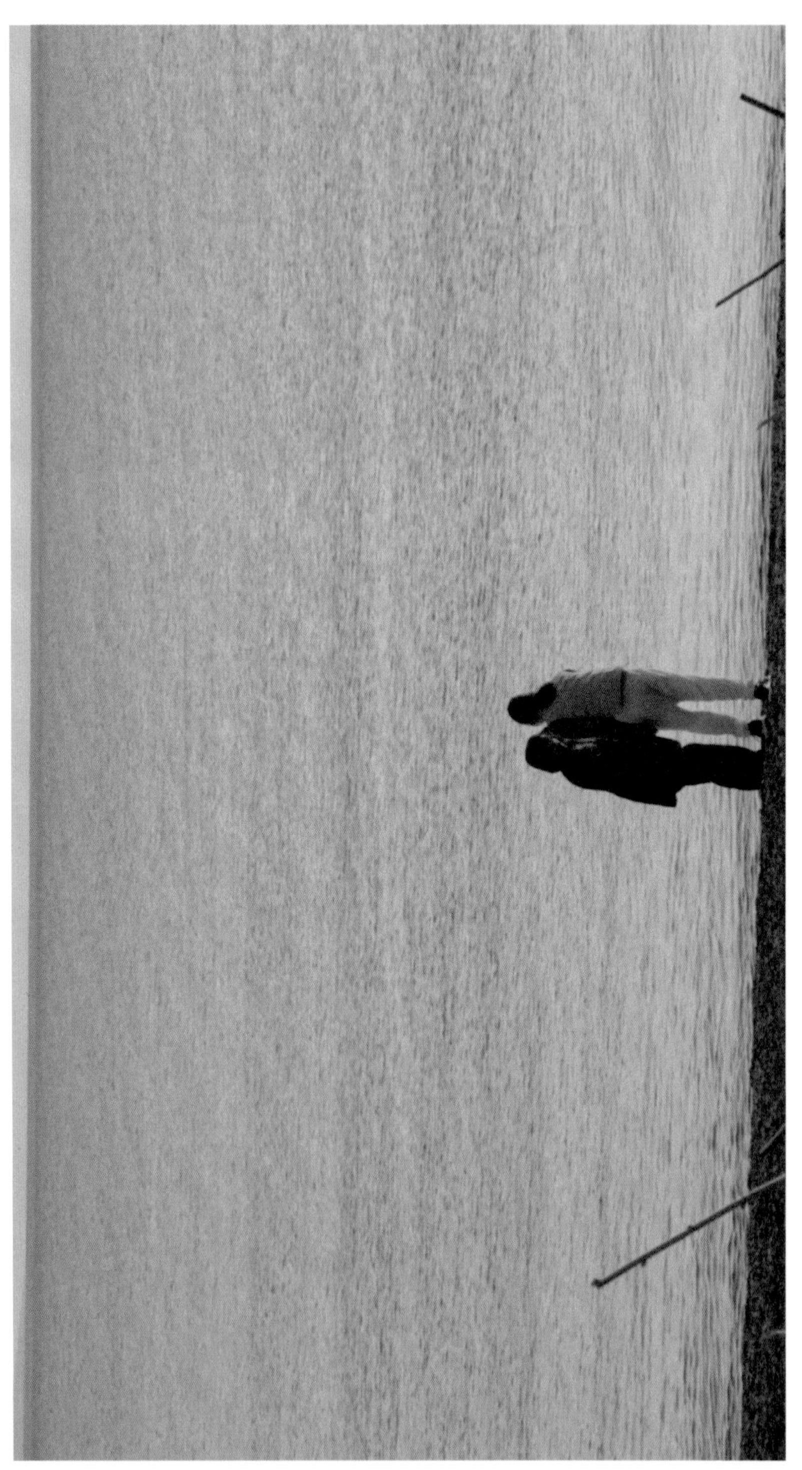

and displaced here and now. Ever-present too is the stalwart crumbling past, and constant mighty fertile Nature.

Via del Mare, in the Sant'Eufemia district, is one such street. You will always find cars pulled up next to the stone fountain of ground water that flows cool and clean, non-stop, from which people fill their plastic bottles for free. Painted on a shop window are simulacra of timeless Americana, sunfaded Disney characters, next to Bangladeshi silver shops, Moroccan grocery stores, a CONAD supermarket, an abandoned gas station, an overpriced gas station, one farm-style villa with floor-to-ceiling wooden balconies that remained shuttered, a construction site adjacent to the long-distance train station, Lamezia Terme Centrale, a couple of cafés that serve sandwiches and arancini of a more than decent quality, the so-called Grand Hotel Lamezia Terme, passion flowers, palms, oleanders, and canes that tower above human height, and on the far side of the station, the truly grand shell of an abandoned sugarbeet processing factory, on the outer wall of which a spray-painted cartoon stork with a speech bubble reads (in Italian) "Humanity has failed."

It is here too, clustered on this stretch of road, that the highest density of Chinese-owned import shops in the region may be found. My collaborator and I set out to meet and document the community of Chinese migrants who run these shops, which are an essential part of Italian domestic life across demographics of race and class. I had imagined we might paint a subtle (perhaps wordless) portrait of people interacting with the reams of objects sold in the import shops of Via del Mare: many sizes of colorful boxes with lids, piled almost to the ceiling, arranged like houses on the side of a mountain, fake flowers, underwear, batteries, hibiscus-shaped hair clips in red and pale blue, Kinder surprise eggs, Goleador candies, gummy candy hamburgers, gum balls, bicycle tires, garbage bags, bug spray, the iconic orange sports balls, light like a balloon but painted to look like a basketball, regular soccer balls, light-up toy dogs, fake guns, stress balls, fidget spinners. And the subtle relations that show up in how a consumer moves through the aisles, how greetings and currency are exchanged, how items get bagged: through this, I thought we could learn something. I thought we might even find someone with an interest in performing, or at least in being on camera—someone who could be our star.

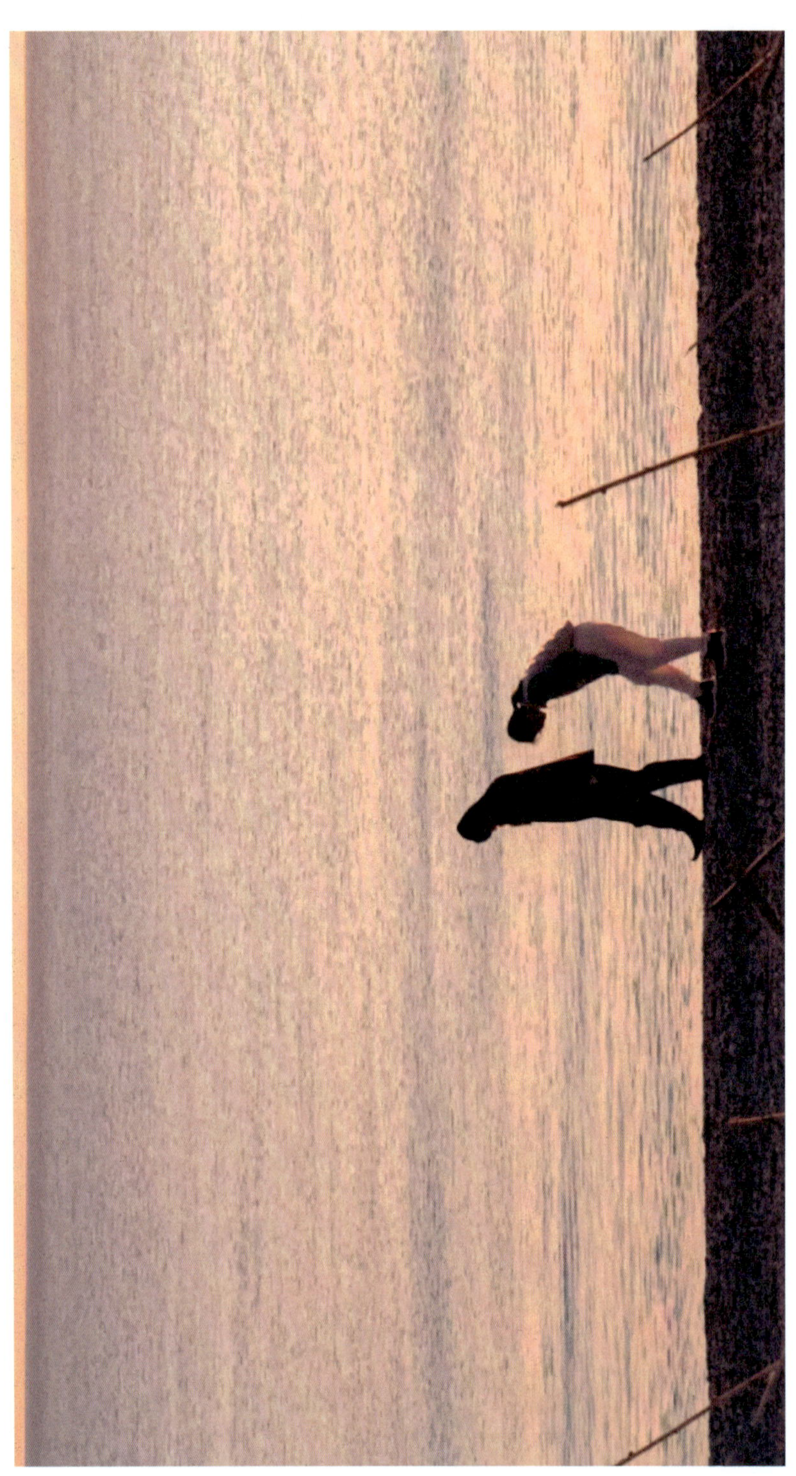

The proprietor of the first store we approach, "Il Sud," a shop selling bags of various sizes and uses, visibly shrinks at the sight of us. My collaborator initiates conversation in Mandarin, but before she can finish one sentence he has already said "No" with a laugh that suggests "No way." There will be no pressing him. And at the next shop, another "No," and another. The three of us in our dark rain jackets, my collaborator and I with cameras, and my partner with his domineering windcaged microphone, cut a more repellant figure than I realized. I am embarrassed at this miscalculation. I start to feel that we might be doing something wrong by even asking. That our desire to learn, to document, whatever, is in fact bad. The fact that we are inquiring makes us a threat, and the images we are suggesting to make will be even more threatening.

I feel a mounting exhaustion at these thoughts, so we stop, have a coffee and some cakes at the Station Bar, reassess, and change our approach. My collaborator would go into the shops alone. I would stay at a distance. She wouldn't ask anyone for anything, she wouldn't introduce our "project," she would just chat, and eventually ask permission to record these chats. This approach proved successful.

05

My collaborator conducted these conversations almost completely independently from then on, with less and less intervention from me as the days passed. Some days, I sat in the car and slept, or raged at my own uselessness, which I twisted into moralisms. "I don't want the basis of this project to be sneaking around!" I rage when my collaborator comes back to the car one day. "Am I speaking into a void? What are we doing?!" I am frustrated because it isn't clear whether my collaborator is following my instructions in my absence: to follow leads and go deep, and tread respectfully, and do justice to individual stories and to the larger political context, to be incisive but empathetic, to dig but to let lie. Whether I was in the car or in the shop, or in the street next to the shop, or in the café by the station, or in my bedroom, the fact was that I was on the outside. There was communication going on, meaningful and purposeful, people were speaking and being understood, but I was not part of that exchange, and I had very little idea about the quality or content of those exchanges.

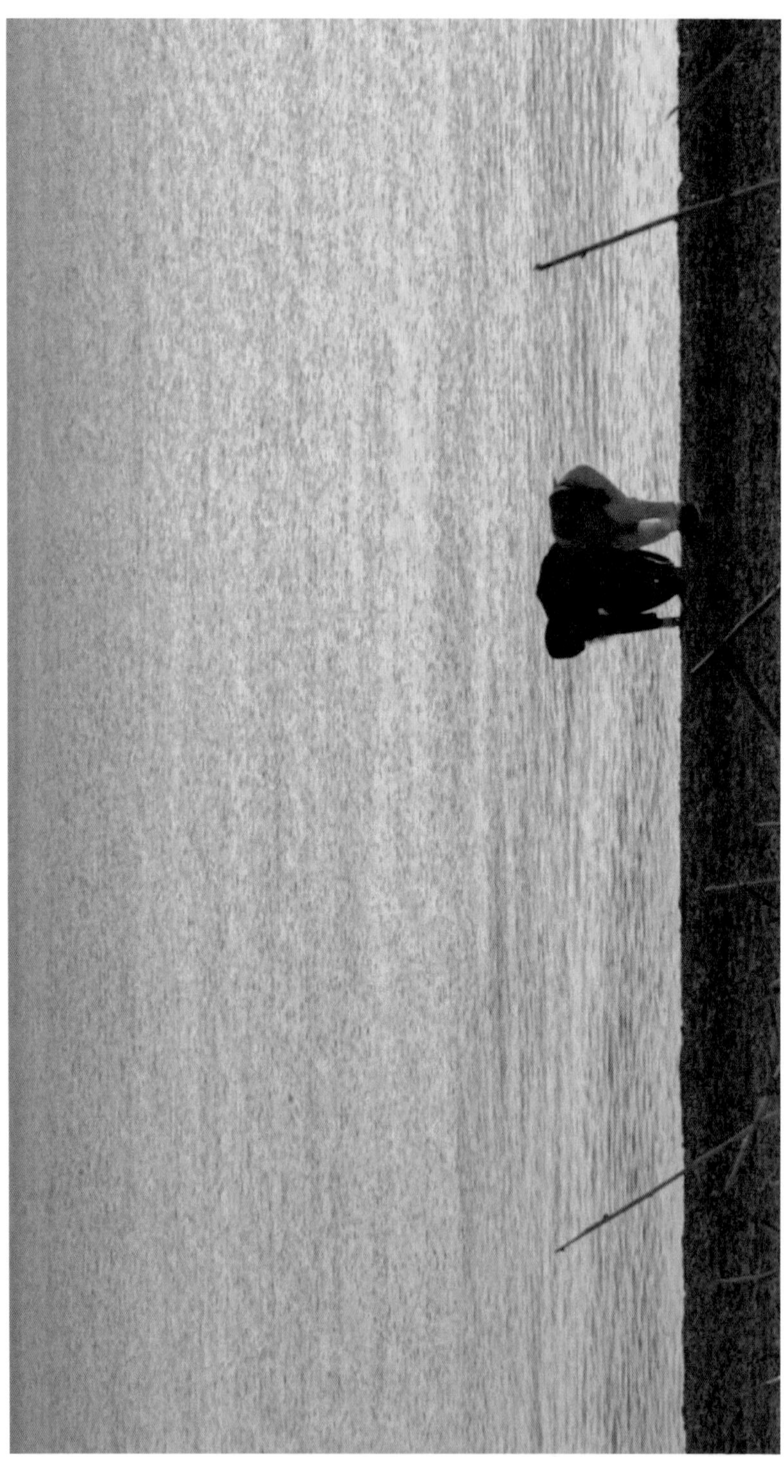

My collaborator would recount the conversations at the end of each day. We would drive through the mountains or along the coast and she would describe her interactions; but her interactions were, by nature, long meandering, spontaneous chats, and the detail and personality that would eventually make them cinematic, relevant, particular, and alive was not something she could summarize; nor was it possible for her to translate that mass of content from day to day, so I could look into it myself and find patterns or direction. I had no idea where we were in our project, or where we were going, and we would anyways have to continue shooting, day after day, and I would have to remain in the dark.

In film, maybe especially in experimental film, there is a fine line between something and nothing. What if we just stayed home today instead of going out filmmaking? What if we work a whole day, a whole many months of days, and have nothing that hits a nerve, lights up? What if the film in its final form, is so diaphanous, so ordinary, as to barely exist. And yet, in the accumulation of moments there is depth, in the particularity of moments there is reality. During this time, I had a dream that large green pears could be something like "cooked" if sunk to the bottom of a river and left there: that the water running over them would make them perfectly evenly soft. Slowly but surely ripening.

I kept thinking that pregnancy felt like the most passive condition of creation; I could not act on this being's behalf; I could not direct its growth; nothing needed to be planned, written, decided; there was a program, a schedule, a script very much in place, and all I could do was tend to myself as its host. I started asking myself at what point the fetus becomes conscious. But I already knew—not because of any perceptible physical sensations (the subtle tapping on the walls, i.e. my body, that his movements began to make around that time), but because of the sudden appearance of a new rending fear of loss, and something like a separate personality present within me—that it was "now"-ish.

There was so much going on inside me. Every few days I needed to retreat to my bedroom in fear and frustration. Weeping for hours. This was simply how my body metabolized pregnancy. I wanted to hide it from my collaborator, but my tears were gargantuan, loud, full-body eruptions. No one could understand what I was feeling and I was desperate to stop feeling it. Because the fetus would be pumped with this same anguish and be damaged; because my collaborator would think I

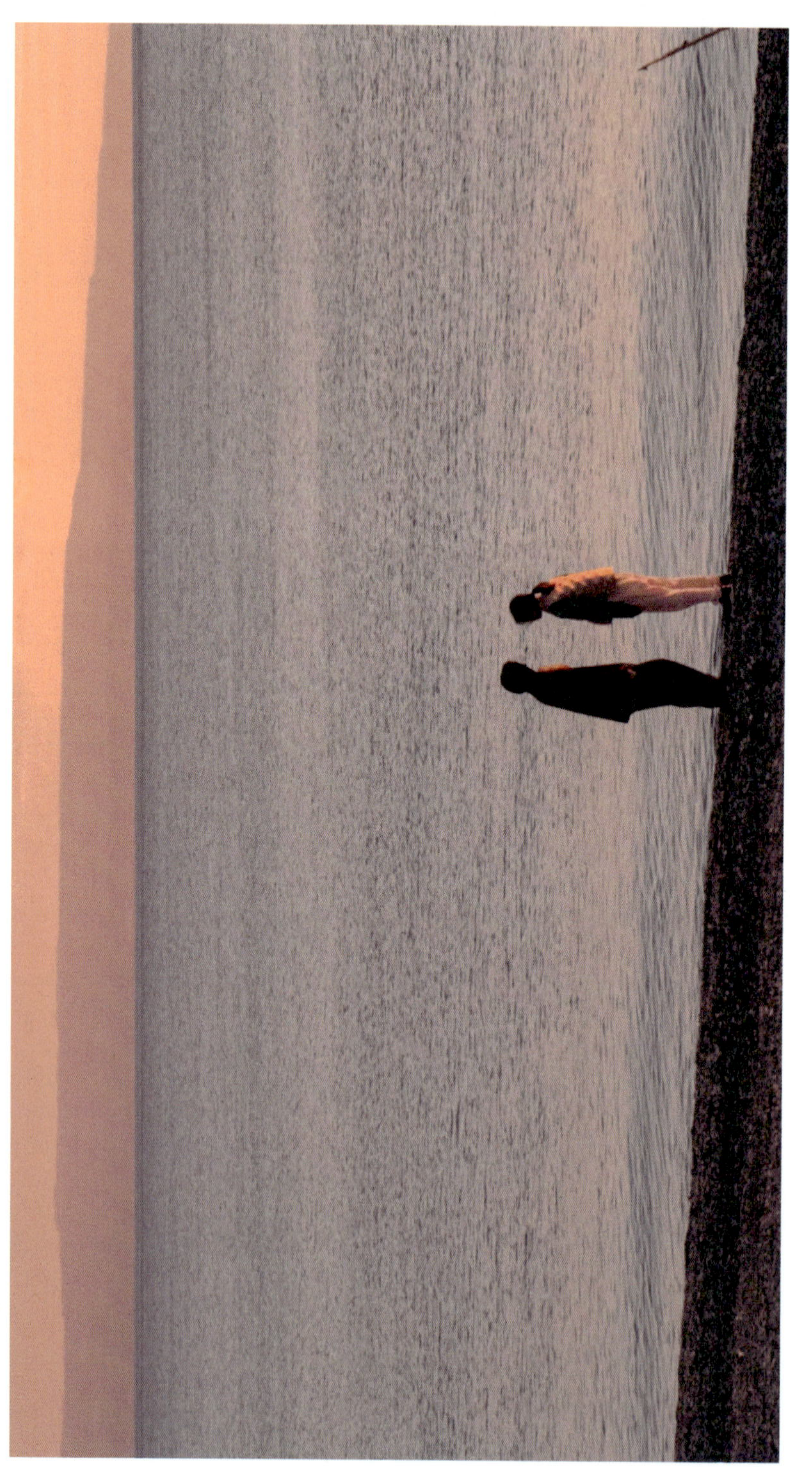

was crying about her. But she always told me, once I had emerged and apologized, "Don't worry, you're doing something very important," and she patted me on the shoulder.

06

These most meaningful moments were not caught on film, and neither was much else. We had almost no images to use. The shop owners explained to my collaborator, who explained to me, that the police in the region hunted the internet for proof that the Chinese-owned shops were not following regulations. One shop owner explains, "The foreigners [the Italians] are strange. They will mostly ignore us, and then suddenly they are paying attention, and they become very strict." So we again reassess our original hypothesis. Because there are good reasons that the shop owners don't want to be seen, which we decide should be reflected in the way we use images in the film, i.e. the way images that represent are selectively absented.

I will note that I did the editing alone, and this was where I did take control. I took the footage, the conversations, the translations and shaped them—but my collaborator was nonetheless present throughout. For one, she had translated all of the conversations from Mandarin to English, which was another kind of control on her part, but even more, I was seeing her activity of the previous weeks in great detail for the first time.

I witnessed her incredible quiet skill. An untroubled, conversational tone, a direct curiosity about others, an ability to find strange relations, bewildering similarities, and this immediately puts her interlocutors at ease. She also has a naïve, almost helpless quality, which may or may not be sincere, and a compulsion to bring the conversation to herself—the wholeness of these qualities gives the film its personality. I see the countless unguarded moments that didn't make it into the film: my collaborator applies Nutella to a cookie with such laborious care, coming at the cookie from various angles, sculpting the Nutella as if with a palette knife. I see the contagion of collaboration take place. I start saying "actually" before most sentences, as my collaborator does. My curiosity shows itself in the same stooped posture, a deep forward lean that my collaborator uses when she stares into the items on the shelves in our house.

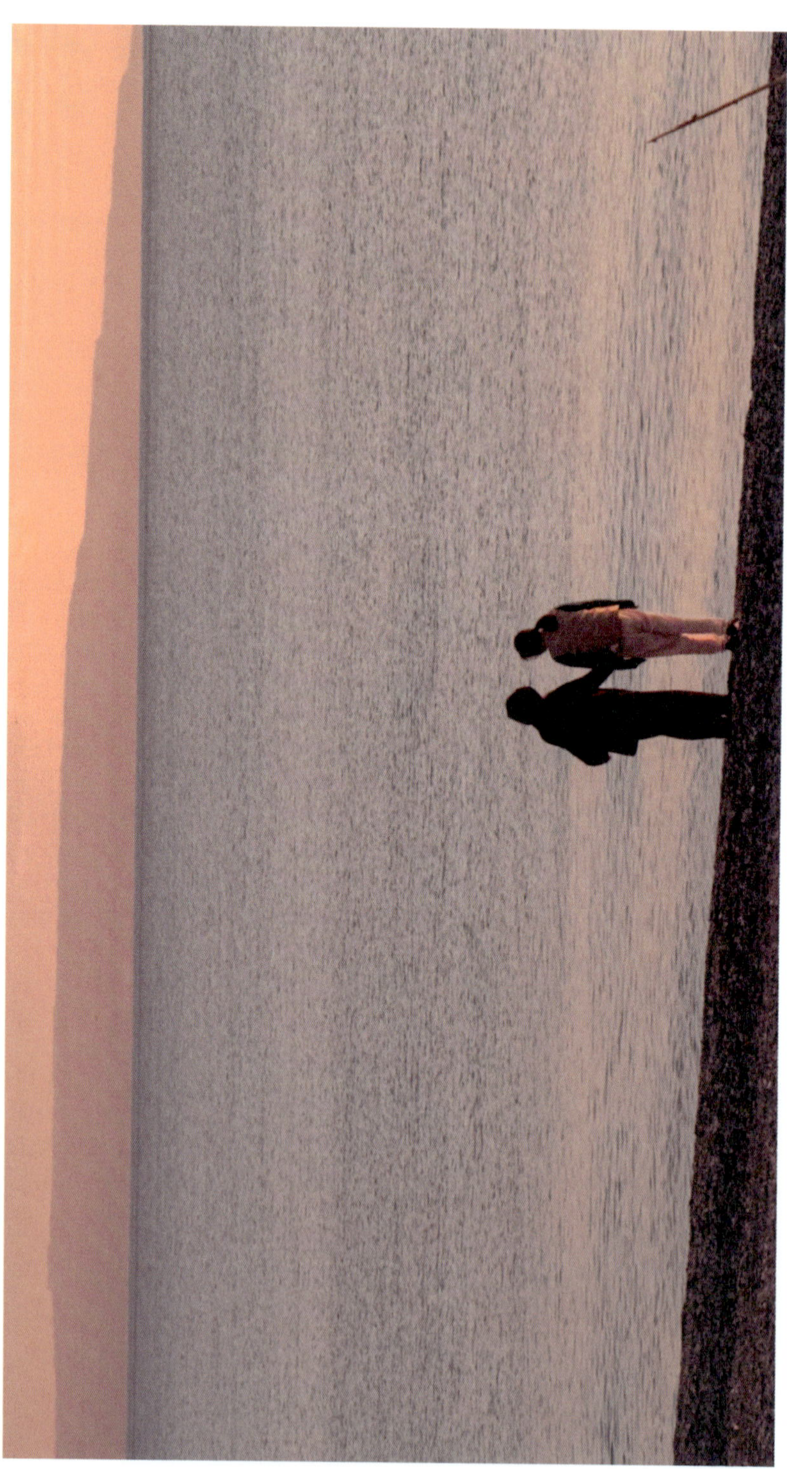

To complete the picture: the visuals we used in the film, in the end, were extreme close-up views of the shops, dark and blurred, that come into focus only in snatches, the camera strapped to the body, moving around with whoever wears it (footage captured first by accident and then repeated), as well as shots of people coming and going from the central station.

07

Being in reality is a practice. When I've really been tested, I've found myself, rodent-like, rummaging for scraps of stories and identities that indicate strength and make sense; because acts of surrender often feel like failure. I had pictured giving birth to my child: I would submit to the pain and let ego-destroying waves of agony wash over me as I became pure being or non-being. I had fantasized about this, even looked forward to it. This had nothing to do with the reality I would live.

Surrender, in my case, looked like letting myself, after suffering through days of excruciating ineffectual work, be laid down on the operating table, legs together, arms outstretched, strapped down by my ankles and wrists in my own passion moment. There is no footage of this phenomenal hour of our lives.

I feel the impulse here and now in language to invoke more of that, which for different reasons I cannot or will not show, which is not only a question of whether the footage exists. We do have footage of the kittens, a tangle under a tarp on the cold floor of the garage, wet with afterbirth, the mother gripping them closer as they nestle into her matted fur for her nipples. The cat looks proud of the work she has done and is doing. We don't know if we intervened too much (bringing a heater into the garage, handling a few of the kittens once they started to show signs of slowed breathing), or not enough (maybe we should have brought them all into the house; it was so cold that April), or perhaps we played no part in what happened. We have footage, too, of the way the cat mourns her loss, takes the bodies of the kittens into hidden places, licks them, and spends time coming into the reality of their death. We have footage of our neighbors' half-built house, down the road from the apartment building where they will continue to live, because they will never finish the house, because they built the facade, they built a turret before the plumbing. We have footage of the cultural liaison of the

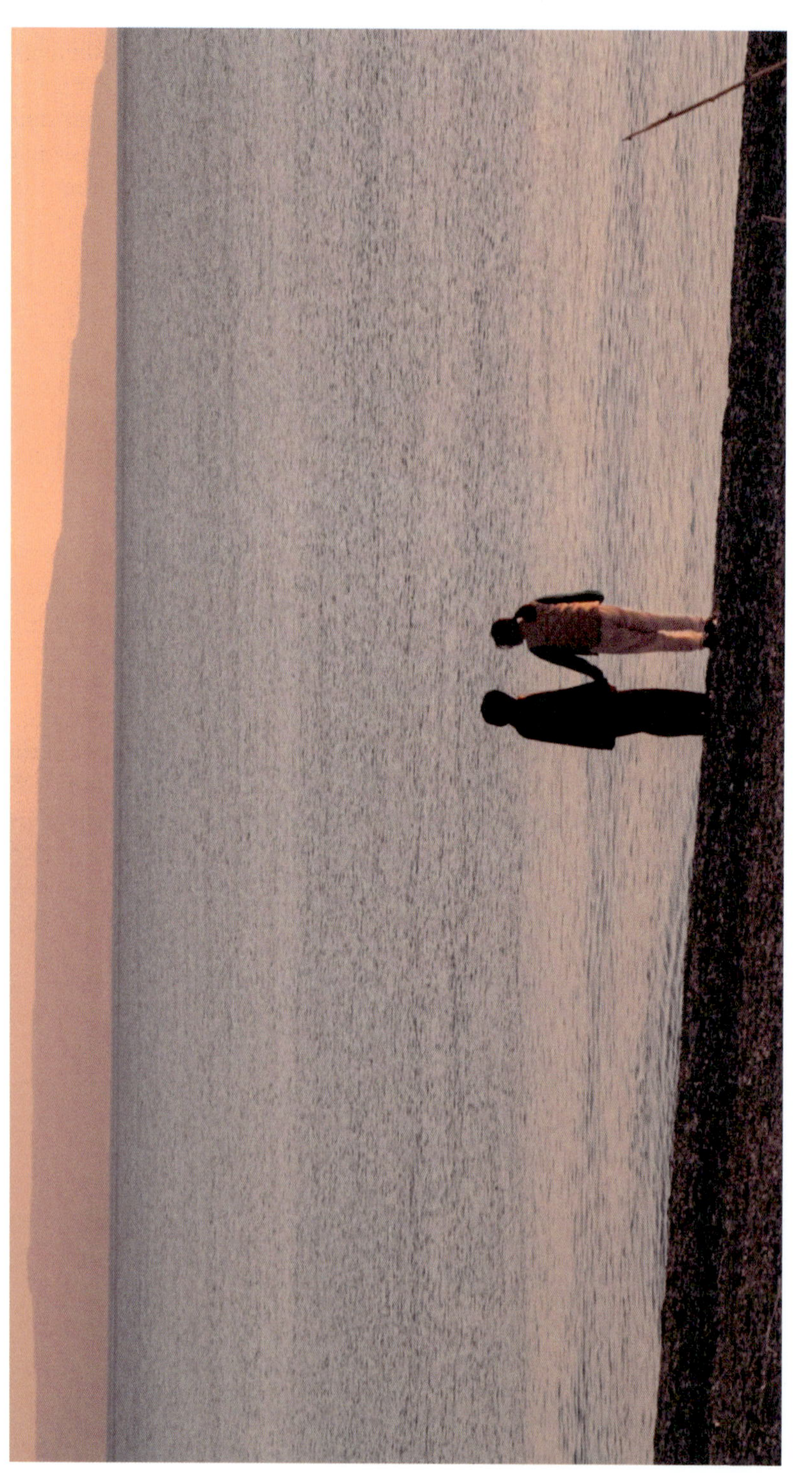

Chinese community telling my collaborator about his views on homosexuality. We have footage of the Chinese Cultural Center on Via Del Mare, which the cultural liaison played a part in starting. We don't have footage of his son, who is there, learning Mandarin. We have footage of an Italian flag, a Chinese flag, the center's meeting room lined with group photos of the Chinese business owners of Lamezia Terme, they are all from Zhejiang, a southeastern province of China. Many of the shop owners that we speak to say that Calabria, the Italian South, feels more like home to them than Milan or Rome, that people are kinder, they thank you if you hold the door open, they acknowledge that you exist. We don't have footage of the expensive seafood dinner that the cultural liaison takes us out to; of his masterful ordering of plates of raw seafood and tripe stew; of my deliberating whether it would be appropriate for me to try to pay. We don't have footage of his family, who joins us, his wife and son, and his two teenage daughters who speak the Calabrese dialect better than I ever will.

I return to this almost-existing feeling. To the question of what it means to hold the responsibility of bringing something into the world, to shepherd it, to make sure it turns out a certain way—lest everything you have put into it comes to nothing, or worse, comes to something that does harm. When I say reality, I mean as opposed to something: to invention, to ideals, to dreams, to expectation, to fiction, to falsity, to the image itself. In filmmaking I aim to make this effort to clear out the mind and look again, over and over, with the question, "What is really going on here?" This applies to footage, once it exists: to let go of the idea of what I thought was happening at the time, in the room, and instead to see what is happening in what is visible, what is to be heard. To let the material lead me somewhere unexpected, to be willing to follow, to be disproven, to be shown to have been foolish, to let a hoped-for thing cease to exist. And then to take on, in whatever manner is called for, what does exist.

A recent winter day in Berlin: bright and crisp, tall square apartment buildings, with wrought iron balcony rails casting sharp angular shadows. I am alone, a very rare thing at the moment, without child or partner, alone with my thoughts, in the street in the cold sunlight. And the spontaneous feeling of reality strikes me—I have a child, that child exists. I have heard the experience repeated by other new parents, that

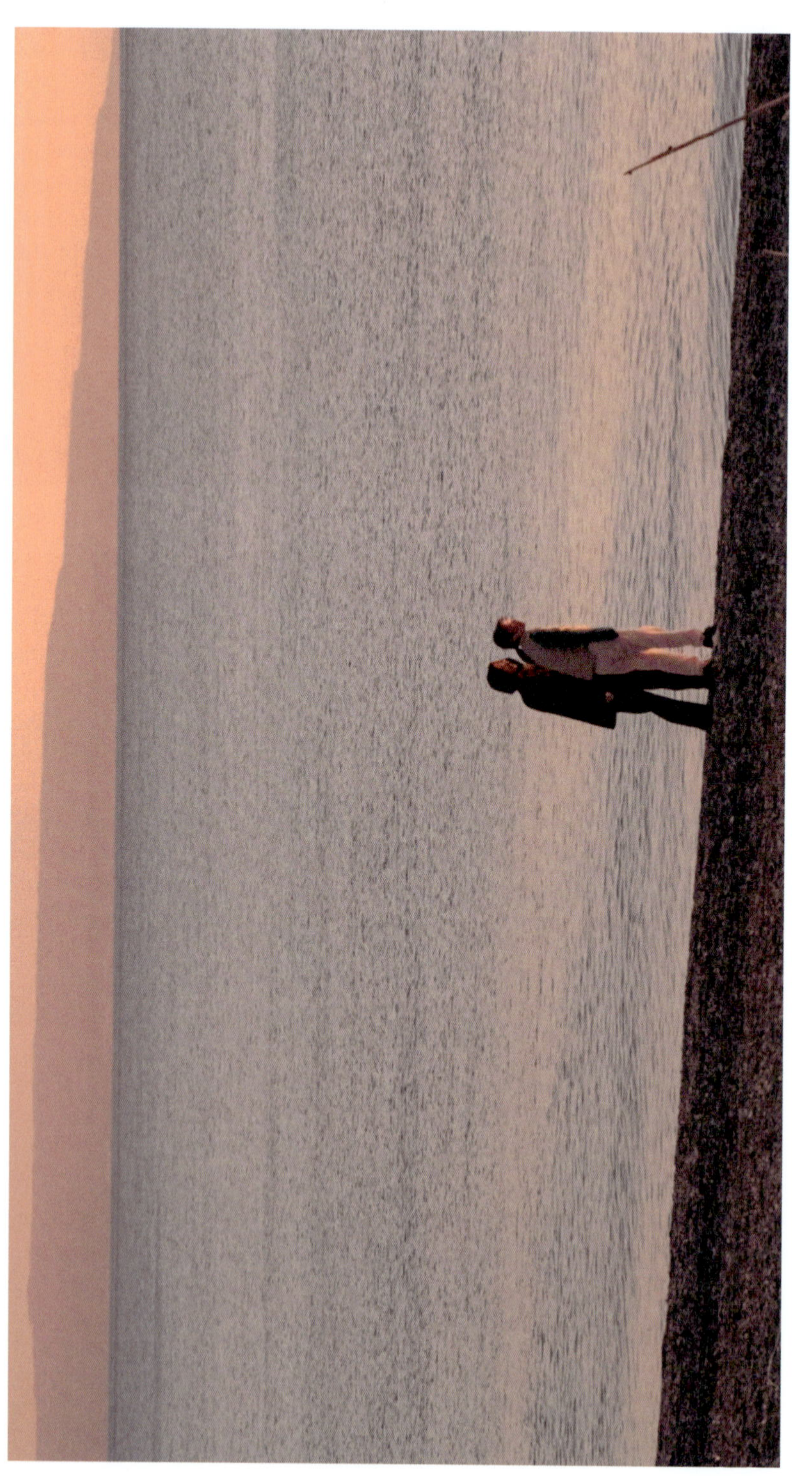

for a long time after birth there is a sense of unreality and abstractness, in part because of the crush of the day-to-day: a new, intense, constant vigilance about another being. It takes time to be able to stick your head out and grasp where you are. It happened again later that day, as he chewed on my finger. I could feel the complexity of the inside of his mouth, his full tongue, like my tongue, and the reality of his internal forms. He put his fingers in my mouth too, and he was pleased—he, not at all an image but a being of complex tissues and responses—a complete interiority, distinct from and yet the same as my own.

Method and Image in Rosa Aiello's Experimental Documentary
Yaniya Lee

I knew Rosa Aiello only vaguely when we ended up together at a residency in the Rocky Mountains of Western Canada. I had an image of her from a previous life, when we had both lived in Montreal and she seemed to always be dipping back, just briefly, into the city after some glamorous adventure abroad. Maybe this is just to say that before I knew her as a sensitive and dedicated artist and collaborator, I thought she was sophisticated and mysterious. I found out filmmaking had become her focus. That year alone, 2017, she had already produced three experimental shorts. At the residency she was working on fiction and an upcoming exhibition, both connected to her family home in Calabria. Each project, she explained, had "to do with my communities there, and my position halfway-in, half-out of this place (which is a nation, a culture, a language, a way of life)."[1]

Rosa and I, along with some of the others in our cohort, formed a Sylvia Wynter reading group. A couple of times a week we met in the sunny boardroom at the back of the Library and Archives Center and read the Jamaican theorist's texts out loud, stopping to discuss as we went. It was a slow process. When taken seriously, Wynter's radical epistemological leaps threaten to overturn the value systems that hold together everything familiar to us. This new way of understanding the power structures, culture, and social and environmental relations gave us an uncomfortable ideological self-awareness that began to change our approach to research and filmmaking, or, as Rosa wrote in an email at the time, "Starting to apply Wynter to my life and it is blowing the top of my head right off. I realize, in many ways, I am addicted to the opiate rewards of staying deep down in the normative order."[2]

The entire length of our stay, forest fires raged, filling the skies with a constant haze. Our cohort put together a special issue of an academic journal themed on "smoke."[3] Rosa and I, buzzing from the new, world-shifting ideas we were reading together, decided to collaborate on an experimental, fragmentary text.[4] It took us months to write. A combination of emails and Skype dates and phone calls generated a Google doc that we both regularly wrote into from our respective sides of the Atlantic (me in Toronto, Rosa in Berlin). We mixed fact and fiction, philosophy and theory, fragments and anecdotes, news and myth. Having disavowed any claim to single authorship, our contributions became an undifferentiated mass. In the end, I couldn't tell what she had put in and what I put in, what was true and what was made up. Blending our contributions in this way, relinquishing control, created the conditions for trust to develop between us.

In the intervening years, collaboration has become an integral part of Rosa's practice. In each new project, she establishes processes and sets up situations that allow her to be responsive to her collaborators' ideas and direction, attentive to the structure that holds these working relationships together. In one interview, also from 2017, Rosa explicitly points to her fascination with structures: "I [want] to admit my ambivalence about structures, my fear of them, embeddedness in them, and fascination with them. I use a loose definition to say what is a structure. I would include language, family, architecture, cities, the gallery, morality, narrative, social roles, education, guilt, taxonomy, duty, to name a few."[5] The potentially radical act of remaking our social relations and changing how power operates in a certain configuration of roles is something that can effectively be done on a small scale, for instance, while making a movie. Just as she had done while writing that collaborative text with me so many years ago, now as a director Rosa has learned to lean away from unilateral authorship. Instead of fixed scripts, she writes outlines and contexts; instead of a meticulous rundown, she prepares a rough sequence of events. This porous way of doing things allows for the unexpected and makes space for the generative potential of the unplanned. "I put myself in situations where I don't feel masterful or in control ... to follow the flow of reality more than to intend and construct."

is as if the process is turned inside out, so the seams can be seen. And the parameters and relations that Rosa sets up to structure the making are revealed as themselves an important part of the final project.

A Good Reputation (2025) is an "improvised fiction" film shot in Calabria with non-actor Giulia Vittoria Maione, Rosa's second cousin by marriage, and professional actor Mackenzie Davis, a longtime friend of Rosa's, who has established herself as a lead in television and cinema. In the first ten minutes of the film, we see looped footage of a descent into a darkened entrance stairwell, overlaid with a conversation between Rosa and Giulia. Giulia, who has just moved into Rosa's passed grandmother's apartment, is giving Rosa a detailed rundown of the local gossip. The man who lives downstairs, a figure who is never seen, is invoked through Giulia's storytelling and through the half-open doors shown in the looped footage. Here, community is connected by people's perceptions of one another. A good or bad reputation is a result of how you are viewed, and the ways in which people talk about you when you're out of sight.

This notion of reputation and the pressure that accompanies it is brought into relief with the arrival of Mackenzie, a celebrity actress from abroad. Although Giulia welcomes Mackenzie into her home, Mackenzie has the persistent feeling she is being judged for doing the wrong thing.

"I had written a series of situations that we would film. And the first situation was Mackenzie arriving at the train station with no one there to meet her … We all know how bad that feels, and that set the tone for the entire shoot. Though it was fictional, it was representative of real dynamics Mackenzie and I were going through to learn how to work together. A sense of searching for how to meet each other in this process. A sense that I was perhaps failing to meet her. We have been intimate friends for over twenty years. We were both terrified that something of the experience of making this film would be disappointing and that that would damage this precious friendship, or harm our elevated views of each other. And that developed into an arc of Mackenzie's attitude toward the experience of being an outsider in Calabria, and in Giulia's home. At first Mackenzie is very cooperative and wants to be involved, wants to behave ... but by the end of the long and drawn out all-day lunch—which is common in the South, but which feels endless for people not used to this kind of durational visiting—she's lost her patience, she's done with trying to understand or fit in."[6]

In the film, the tension between Rosa's methods and Mackenzie's expectations as an actress are palpable. Added to this is the way Mackenzie's character, who speaks only English, is made alternately extremely vulnerable and almost invisible in the context of Rosa's family, who speaks only Italian. Mackenzie develops a heightened awareness of how they see, or fail to see her. This had not necessarily been a part of Rosa's plan:

"I thought that I could act as their translator but in the end, it was harder than I thought to do that ... It was of course more than translating what one woman says to the other—there is a whole raft of unspoken subtleties and social expectations that are too intangible to explain, too weighed down by my own family histories and hierarchies. ... I was also genuinely concerned with how my cousins would experience the film shoot, that we might do something to offend them. I was probably more concerned with their comfort than Mackenzie's, and that showed. At the end Mackenzie makes some kind of refusal by leaving the apartment and performing a monologue—which was the most actorly, agential thing we could think for her to do."[7]

As a viewer, it's hard to know how much of this tension is orchestrated and how much is organic. This uncertainty, where we don't, while watching, know what is real and what isn't, is the manifestation on screen of Rosa's carefully orchestrated method.

Problems of visibility, reputation, translation, and collaborative intimacy are also at play in the multi-channel film *Interface or: The Daily Pressure of Watching* (2025), an experimental documentary about the Chinese shop owners and workers in the wholesale district of Lamezia Terme, made with artist Yutong Su. Yutong asks the Chinese shopkeepers in Calabria to share their experience on film. Though they agree to participate and tell their stories, they don't want to be captured on camera. For them, as a Chinese diaspora in Italy, whose difference is worn on the skin, there is a vulnerability to being seen. Their image captured on video could become a danger to them, and so the documentary shifts into an act of storytelling using barely legible images. We hear the speakers continually, and we see handheld close-up views of the shelves and products of shops, where the shopkeepers spend their days. Rosa, present as director, doesn't understand these conversations in the moment, only later, after Yutong translates them, will she know what was said. When conceiving of this film with Yutong, Rosa had been influenced by Agnes Varda's 1976 documentary *Daguerreotypes*:

"... about the shopkeepers of the street that she lived on for twenty-five years. She makes snapshot portraits of people that run the shops. In a way, [*Interface*] is a failed version of that film. My naïveté, or my failure, was in misunderstanding the politics of visibility and the relationship between disclosure and intimacy. I was just meeting the shop owners: I hadn't been living on this street for twenty-five years, and their vulnerability to being seen was a completely different thing than that of French shop owners in a French village. They're a Chinese immigrant group doing semi-legal retail businesses in supposedly wholesale shops, and they don't want their goods to be seen, and they don't want their faces to be seen, and they don't want their customers to be seen. So a lot of this process was coming to understand their position in the broader social structure."[8]

For both films, Rosa shot adjacent material and set up an "infrastructure in order to accumulate things around the edges," she explained. "When you're filmmaking and the image isn't the goal, or the image is itself problematic, what forms the visual field [when] you know you are still working in a medium of images? I found that this sort of almost-image or barely-there image is a way of creating mood and movement and space. So [then] mood, movement and space [take precedence] over figures or representation or faces, or other kinds of things that are tied to identities,"[9] she says. "Bits and pieces may then become central. For example, the looped footage at the beginning of *A Good Reputation* was not a planned shot, but was filmed because I turned on my camera on my way out of the apartment at the end of a shooting day."[10]

The filmmakers Rosa admires have a tendency to take a rough approach, to challenge the cinematic conventions that usually demand a lot of polish. So much of the apparatus and method and scheduling of cinema is about capturing an image that is beautiful and exceptional and continuous. But this can happen at the expense of everything else. "I prefer to prioritize the emotion and whatever one might call the realness of a moment over the perfection of the image. And for me those two things are really in opposition to each other since the image—the perfect image, even in documentary—requires so much contriving and effort, and then you're taking your attention away from the actual situation or the moment or the encounter that's in front of you."[11] Rosa is interested in making processes for herself, not images. Her attention to the entire realm of relationships that make up production is exercised in careful and complex preplanning and preparation. This lays a relational ground for production, she says, "to allow the work that I'm making, or myself, to be influenced and led by a situation, an impulse, a person, an accident, a limitation."[12] The film is, for her, an apparatus that produces possibilities of encounter and engagement outside of ordinary life: "I don't feel like the film that I make needs to represent at all what that experience was."[13] Again, neither evidence, nor representation, but a trace nonetheless.

This approach comes with a concern for her with respect to the boundaries of collaboration. If the shared goal around which all participants have gathered and labored is to create moving images, is it justifiable for her to be seeking something beyond those images? Is this a question of transparency about a final product, or are all image-production processes laden with this kind of duplicity? In another essay, I wrote that "image representation can ... obfuscate the social relations that exist beyond the frame."[14] And yet, the image is always also entangled with the context of its production, and can even risk becoming misaligned with its interpretive context. According to filmmaker Bill Nichols, "Images can indeed provide a form of authentication regarding something anterior to themselves ... but the surrounding frames, contexts, narrative structures, televisual forms, viewer assumptions, and expectations vie with one another. They constitute, in aggregate, a social arena devoted to interpretative struggle."[15]

There is a history of this kind of making in experimental film and documentary. Rosa is part of a filmmaking tradition that prioritizes situation or method, or the development of a set of relationships over the final image. William Greaves's *Symbiopsychotaxiplasm: Take One* (1971), for instance, has become a legendary part of the experimental documentary film canon. As director, writer, editor, and co-producer, Greaves orchestrated a story within a story in the style of direct cinema. He had an unconventional way of filmmaking: he set up the conditions for all participants and parts of the process to be observed, and in a way, to simultaneously orchestrate three films in one. "In *Take One,* Greaves auditioned acting students for a fictional drama (called *Over the Cliff*), while simultaneously shooting the camera crew that was filming the audition, and then filming those filmmakers with a third camera crew."[16] Greaves wanted something of the real of the actors and crew to come through, he felt that their performances would be more true if he could adjust the structure, manipulate the form. In one sense, Greaves's deception could be seen as manipulating his crew, but in another, he was orchestrating a structure, a situation, into which a certain kind of revelation could emerge, something intangible, organic, and true.

Harun Farocki has observed how techniques of imaging and methods of filming can, in themselves, be the maneuver that lends authenticity to the story. In other words, it's not what is seen but how it is captured that matters. He talks about the relationship between the actors' movements in a scene and how the cameraman films the action. "In feature films—classic feature films—the camera anticipates. In the documentary, the camera pursues. In the classical feature film, the camera knows the staging—the screenplay, the construction plans for the studio ... The camera knows the production text and speaks it without faltering. This fluency corresponds to the continuity that applies to the sequence of shots."[17] As he explains: "We documentarians often make Direct Cinema films. We look for events that occur as if they had been staged for a film. At the same time, we have to prove that we have found something and recorded it without writing or staging it."[18] Farocki describes these practices as "controlled uncertainties."

By deconstructing conventions with her methodology, Rosa puts the people in her projects, her collaborators, into situations where their implicit role within a structure is made explicit. Who they are in relation to each other, and how they are defined by their environments surges into sharp relief. Rosa's approach exposes the structure that connects them. The films show how images themselves are not evidence of anything, but rather the trace of something. (Like Mackenzie's vulnerability, or Yutong's lynchpin position.) By deconstructing and remaking the process of creating moving images, Rosa undermines the weight of the final image—instead of constructing a story, she exposes it. I recognize in this an echo of the collaborative writing we did together. What emerged from that process of slow and steady accumulation wasn't a single constructed argument, but rather a unique set of fragments that together created a whole we could never have planned.

I, too, have been thinking a lot about the image. I have been trying to understand the limits of representation, the ethics of the image, the extent of the good it can bring. I have come to the conclusion that we don't need the images. As Katherine McKittrick proposes:

"What it feels like is good enough."[19] There is something significant in the methodology Rosa has developed for producing film—that how we are together, how we bring self-awareness and attention to how we do things, is an ethic and a practice that can generate possibilities, and reveal truths that would otherwise be shut down by our commitment to existing structures and ways of doing, by what we already know and expect. That's boring. That's letting the story be told in advance. When the focus of the artwork is the experience of its making, you end up with a shift in perspective. By changing how we do things, we change the kinds of stories we can tell.

1 Elena Bordignon, "Interview with Rosa Aiello—Fate Presto, Casa Masaccio," ATP Diary (2017), https://atpdiary.com/interview-with-rosa-aiello-fate-presto-casa-masaccio/, accessed May 14, 2026.
2 Rosa Aiello, email message to Yaniya Lee, August 3, 2017, "Wynter Reading Group" email thread (unpublished correspondence).
3 Cf. Rosa Aiello, Nataleah Hunter-Young, and Michael Litwack, eds., "Smoke Figures / Genres / Forms," *Public* 29, no. 58 (Fall 2018): pp. 169–76, https://publicjournal.ca/product/58-smoke-figures-genres-forms/, accessed May 14, 2026.
4 "ON FIRE—Notes on the Spread of a Non-deterministic Schema," co-written text, *Public* 29, no. 58 (Fall 2018): pp. 169–76, eds. Rosa Aiello, Nataleah Hunter-Young, and Michael Litwack, https://publicjournal.ca/product/58-smoke-figures-genres-forms/, accessed May 14, 2026. The introductory paragraph reads: "OUR INTEREST IN FIRE comes from a desire to reveal those structures of geography that are not intrinsic to earth, but which use the idea of the intrinsic to secure and maintain power over territories. This 'cartographic impulse'—the inclination to map, to rationalize, to appropriate, to own, and thereby to control space—treats colonial, exploitative construction as essential, natural, and certain. We are attracted to fire because it has the capacity to lend life to human certainties, that of the map, of the measurement, of the document, of the deed, of the border, because fire respatializes our built environment; because fire is demonic."
5 Bordignon, "Interview with Rosa Aiello."
6 Yaniya Lee, referencing a personal conversation with Rosa Aiello (2025).
7 Ibid.
8 Ibid.
9 Ibid.
10 Ibid.
11 Ibid.
12 Ibid.
13 Ibid.

14 Yaniya Lee, "We Don't Need Images: What It Feels Like Is Good Enough," in *MOMENTA Biennale d'art contemporain: In Praise of the Missing Image* (Bielefeld, 2025), p. 123.

15 Bill Nichols, "'Getting to Know You...': Power, Knowledge and the Body," in *Theorizing Documentary*, ed. Michael Renov (New York, 1993), p. 190.

16 Alison Nastasi, "50 Essential African-American Independent Films," *Flavorwire*, February 16, 2015, https://www.flavorwire.com/504549/50-essential-african-american-independent-films, accessed May 14, 2026.

17 Harun Farocki, "On the Documentary," *e-flux* 65 (May 2015), https://www.e-flux.com/journal/65/336675/on-the-documentary/, accessed May 14, 2026.

18 Farocki, "On the Documentary."

19 Katherine McKittrick, "Something that exceeds all efforts to definitively pin it down," in *Dear Science and Other Stories* (Durham, 2021), p. 74.

Author's Biographies

Beatrice Gibson (b. 1978 GB, lives and works in Palermo, IT) is a French-British filmmaker. Her films are known for their experimental and emotive nature. She has screened her work at numerous museums and festivals, including Fondazione Prada, Milan, IT; Centre Pompidou, Paris, FR; Tate Modern and Tate Britain, London, GB; Highline New York, Light Industry and Anthology Film Archives, New York, US; Cannes Film Festival, Cannes, FR; New York Film Festival, New York, US; Toronto International Film Festival, Toronto, CA. In 2018, she co-founded the bi-monthly film club *The Machine That Kills Bad People* at ICA Cinema, London, GB, alongside Ben Rivers, Maria Palacios Cruz and Erika Balsom. In 2021 she founded *Nuova Orfeo*, an independent platform for experimental cinema and music based in Palermo, IT.

Rosa Aiello (b. 1987 CA, lives and works in Berlin, DE) is an artist, filmmaker, and writer. Her works, at once intimate and alienating, primarily take the form of time-based media: experimental films, architectural installation as well as photographic series. She is interested in structures; both social constructs, like the family, and the actual built world, like city infrastructure. Her most recent solo exhibitions include Westfälischer Kunstverein, Münster, DE, 2025; Mint, Stockholm, SE, 2024; Anorak e.V, Berlin, DE, 2023; Kevin Space, Vienna, AT, 2022. Her works have been shown at Kasseler Dokfest, Kassel, DE; Matatabi Moving Image, Tokyo, JP; Centre Pompidou, Paris, FR; Fluentum and Cittipunkt, Berlin, DE; Institute of Contemporary Arts, London, GB; Whitney Museum for American Art and SculptureCenter, New York, US, among others.

Helin Çelik (b. 1991 TR, lives and works in Vienna, AT) is a Kurdish interdisciplinary artist and filmmaker who investigates different geographies of political struggle, reconstructing existing narratives by interweaving fiction and nonfiction. She strives to unpack the relationship between political and cinematographic memory, by blending personal history and using new visual grammars, aiming to diversify the possibilities of media-making to envision another future. She directed films, including *HABĀ* (2024), *ANQA* (2023) and *What the Wind Took Away* (together with Martin Klingenböck, 2017). Her documentary *ANQA* was shown at Internationale Filmfestspiele Berlin (Berlinale), Berlin, DE; International Film Festival, Gijon, ES; MIRAGE Film Festival for the Art of the Real, Oslo, NO.

Yaniya Lee draws on narratives of liberation to develop new methodologies for art criticism, art history, and archival practice. She is the author of *Selected Writing on Black Canadian Art* (2024, figure ground/Art Metropole) and *Buseje Bailey: Reasons Why We Have to Disappear Every Once in a While, A Black Art History Project* (2024, Artexte).

Ivana Mladenović (b. 1984 RS, lives and works in Bucharest, RO) is an actress and filmmaker. Her first feature documentary *Turn Off the Lights* (2012) premiered at the Tribeca Film Festival, New York, US and won the *Heart of Sarajevo* for Best Documentary, as well as the *Gopo Award* for Best Romanian Documentary. She then directed her first fiction feature, *Soldiers. Story from Ferentari* (2017), based on the autobiographical novel by Adrian Schiop. In 2019, she directed *Ivana the Terrible*, inspired by her own life and filmed with her family and friends; it won the Special Jury Prize at Locarno Film Festival, Locarno, CH, and screened at more than 50 festivals worldwide. Her latest feature *Sorella di Clausura* (2025) premiered in the main competition at Locarno Film Festival, Locarno, CH, and won Best Director at the Sarajevo Film Festival, Sarajevo, BA.

Theresa Roessler (b. 1992 DE) is a curator and writer currently serving as artistic and managing director of the Westfälischer Kunstverein in Münster, DE (since 2024). Her recent projects there include the performance-based exhibition *Basically* by Nikima Jagudajev; solo exhibitions by Eve Tagny, Rosa Aiello, Julia Heyward and Steffani Jemison; as well as collaborations with Peggy Ahwesh, Olga Hohmann, and Sanna Helena Berger. From 2020 to 2023, she was a curator at Kunstverein Freiburg, Freiburg, DE. Her independent curatorial projects include *Taking Notes*, presented at SOPHIE TAPPEINER, Vienna, AT, 2023, as well as Fatima Moallim's first exhibition in Austria at tart.vienna/Galerie Thoman, Vienna, AT, 2024. She also contributes regularly to magazines and exhibition catalogues.

At Night **Writers' Room**

Denna Cartamkhoob is a British-Iranian producer and filmmaker based in London. She has been working predominantly with artists since 2017 in both a production and development capacity. From 2012 to 2017 she worked as an in-house producer at the production company Somesuch. She has also made a number of her own documentaries and has run a virtual writing group for women since 2020.

Amy Gwatkin is a photographer, filmmaker, writer, and electrician. She lives in Kent.

Xiaolu Guo is a Chinese-born British author, filmmaker, and academic. Her writing and films explore migration, alienation, feminism, translation, and transnational identities. Her books include *Village of Stone, A Concise Chinese-English Dictionary for Lovers, I Am China, A Lover's Discourse, Nine Continents and Once Upon A Time In The East,* which received the National Book Critics Circle Award. Guo has also directed a dozen award-winning films, including *She, A Chinese* and *UFO in Her Eyes.* She lives in London.

Sophie Robinson is a poet, novelist, and non-fiction writer. She is the author of *Rabbit* (2018) and *Prairie Oyster* (2026). She lives in London.

Acknowledgments

Matthias Kliefoth would like to thank Rosa Aiello, Helin Çelik, Beatrice Gibson, Yaniya Lee, and Ivana Mladenović.

Rosa Aiello would like to thank Pitt Wenninger, Dylan Aiello, Theresa Roessler, Laura Langer, Elisa R. Linn, Yutong Su, Johanna Markert, Luzie Meyer, Vivien Kämpf, Bitsy Knox, and Mara Zigler.

Image Credits

pp. 14–32
Film stills, *ANQA* (2023), Helin Çelik and Kepler Mission Films

pp. 36–56
Film stills, *Soldiers: Story from Ferentari* (2017), Ivana Mladenović, Luchian Ciobanu, Ada Solomon, and HiFilm Romania

pp. 80–98
Behind the scenes of *Interface or: The Daily Pressure of the Watching* (2025), Pitt Wenninger

KONTEXT – a series by DISTANZ.

Room Tone was initiated on the occasion of Rosa Aiello's solo exhibition *A Good Reputation* at Westfälischer Kunstverein (15.11.2025–1.2.2026), curated by Theresa Roessler.

Imprint

Editors
Matthias Kliefoth, Theresa Roessler

Design
Mali Wychodil

Design Concept KONTEXT
Manuel Tayarani

Text
Rosa Aiello, Helin Çelik, Beatrice Gibson, Yaniya Lee, Ivana Mladenović

Proofreading
Katherine Lewald

Image Editing
max-color, Berlin

Production
Marcus Sabsch

Printing and Binding
Druckhaus Sportflieger, Berlin

ISBN 978-3-95476-798-4

Printed in Germany

Published by
DISTANZ Verlag
www.distanz.de

With support of

Ministerium für
Kultur und Wissenschaft
des Landes Nordrhein-Westfalen

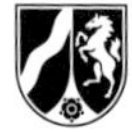

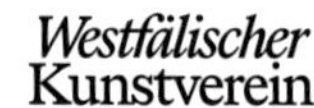